THE CHANGING WORLD OF MONGOLIA'S NOMADS

THE CHANGING WORLD OF MONGOLIA'S NOMADS

Photography and Text by
Melvyn C. Goldstein and Cynthia M. Beall

University of California Press
Berkeley and Los Angeles

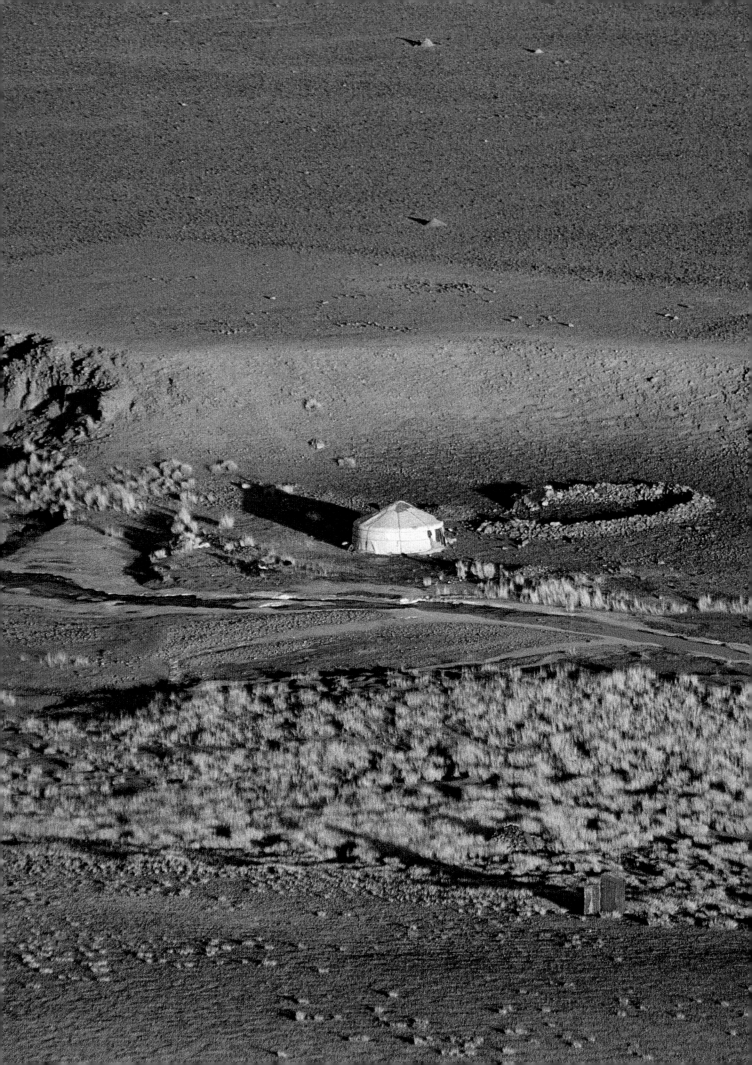

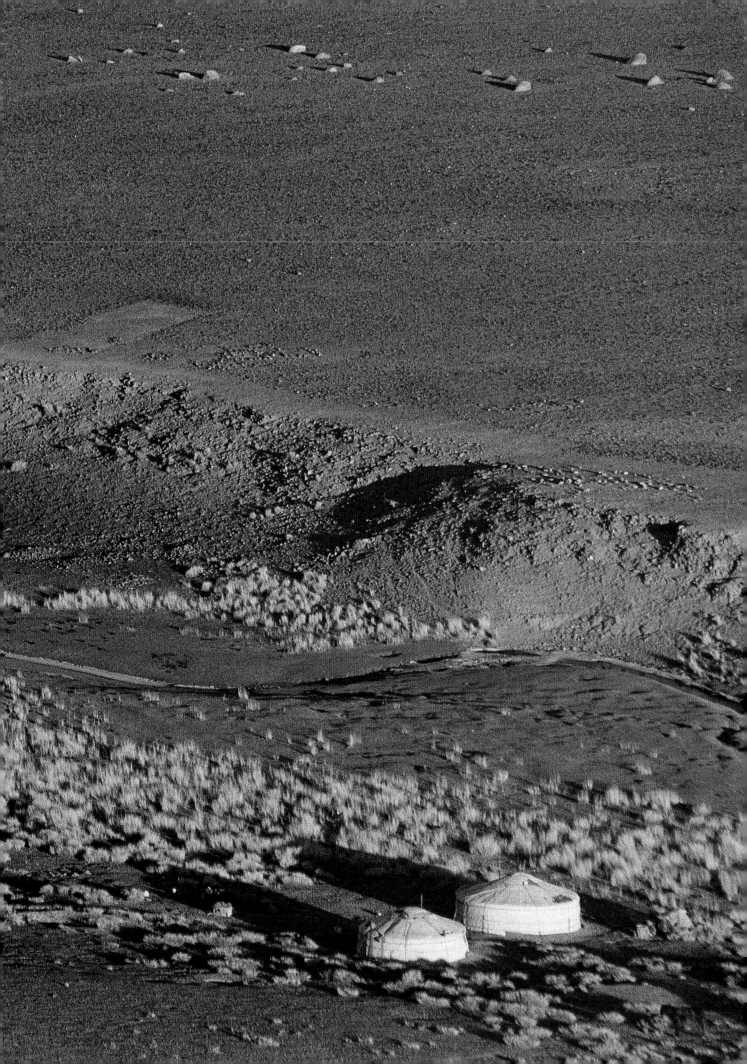

University of California Press
Berkeley and Los Angeles
Published 1994 in North and South America
by the University of California Press

LIBRARY OF CONGRESS CATALOGING-IN-PUBLICATION DATA

Goldstein, Melvyn C.
  The Changing World of Mongolia's Nomads / by Melvyn C. Goldstein
  and Cynthia M. Beall.
     p. cm.
  Includes bibliographical references and index.
  ISBN 0-520-08551-5
  1. Nomads—Mongolia. 2. Collective farms—Mongolia.
  3. Animal industry—Mongolia.   I. Beall, Cynthia M. II. Title.
  DS798.4.G65   1994   93-24004
  951.7—dc20

Designed by David Hurst
Maps courtesy of the National Geographic Society
Production House: Twin Age Limited, Hong Kong
Printed in China
9 8 7 6 5 4 3 2 1

photos (pages 2~3) Cross-country horseracing, wrestling, and archery are Mongolia's three most popular sports. Young children ranging from about age 7 to 13 are typically recruited as jockeys since this allows the race to be a test of the horses rather than their riders.

(page 4) Herders cut hay in summer for emergency use in winter and spring. The supplies are limited, however, and can tide herds over for just a few days.

(pages 6~7) Living in a vast empty land, it is surprising that families will often pitch their ger close together.

(opposite) As their ancestors did in the days of Chinggis Khan, Mongolia's nomads depend on their sturdy horses for transportation. Herders think nothing of riding 5 to 10 miles to visit a friend or relative.

(page 12) War medals commemorating participation in the 1939 battle of Halhyn Gol, where the Mongolians soundly defeated the Japanese, decorate the chest of this pensioner enjoying a quiet smoke.

*Two young children help each other
carrying a pan of dung for fuel.*

PREFACE

MONGOLIA IS ONE OF THOSE CURIOUSLY ANOMALOUS COUNTRIES THAT IS KNOWN BY virtually everyone, but only in terms of an ancient stereotype. Mention Mongolia, and what comes to mind are images of fierce, bloodthirsty hordes of hard-riding nomads, not socialist herders living in collectives in a welfare state. Yet until 1992, the latter was as true as the former.

This, of course, is not surprising, given the dearth of firsthand information about Mongolia. Throughout its 70-year history, Mongolia's communist government adhered to strict Marxist-Leninist ideology and refused to allow Western scholars to conduct fieldwork.[1]

We first learned of an easing of this policy in 1988 while we were living in a Tibetan nomad camp at 17,100 feet.[2] It was an extraordinarily stormy night, with wind and hail battering the encampment, and we had retired to our tent to keep warm and listen to the nightly 10 p.m. Voice of America "Asia Report." Huddled in our sleeping bags with the radio at full volume, we heard a report about Mongolia's incipient glasnost, and about the plans of the United States and Mongolia to begin economic and cultural ties. Later, after the roar of the storm died down, we discussed whether this meant that in-depth anthropological field research in Mongolia would finally be possible. We thought it did and decided to try to secure permission as soon as we were back in the States.

On returning to our university, we found we were right and applied to the U.S.-Mongolia research program that had just been created under the auspices of the International Research and Exchange Organization (IREX). We were selected in 1989 and arrived in Mongolia in 1990. Our aim was twofold—to live with a community of herders and study how they had fared under Marxist collectives and to observe how they were adapting to Mongolia's decision to transform itself into a democratic nation with a market economy.

This book, therefore, is about the life of a community of Mongolian nomads, but it is also the story of how one of the great events of the 20th century—the demise of Russian-style communism—is playing out in nomad camps in the heart of Central Asia.

Because so little has been written about the life of Mongolia's nomads, we have tried to make the book accessible to nonspecialists by using a narrative style that is devoid of academic jargon and the highly technical discussions typical of journal articles and monographs. We have also added images to help bring the people and their mountain environment to life.

---

1. Dr. Dan Rosenberg's brief study-tour in the 1970s was a notable exception to this research blackout, but even then, his research access was circumscribed.

2 . We were conducting the research that resulted in the *National Geographic* article "The Remote World of Tibet's Nomads" (June, 1989) and a book titled *Nomads of Western Tibet: The Survival of a Way of Life* (University of California Press, 1990).

CONTENTS

INTRODUCTION

Our first close-up look at the nomads of Mongolia's Altai Mountains came in September 1990 while en route to Tsaganburgas, a herding camp in Moost district deep in the heart of Central Asia. It was the time of year that Mongols call *altan namar* (golden autumn) the season when the vegetation withers and turns the landscape a golden hue.

As our truck crossed a ridge and descended the rough dirt road onto a broad plain, two herders on horses not much bigger than American ponies emerged from a ravine, driving hundreds of sheep across our path. They rode grandly, integral extensions of their horses, as they fluidly darted back and forth constraining stragglers and urging the herd forward. Their effortless skill reminded us that we had come to this remote place because these were the descendants of the brilliant Mongol nomad cavalry who had terrorized much of Eurasia 750 years earlier, conquering a vast empire that stretched from the Pacific Ocean to the Danube River.

But for the sudden death of their emperor, the ancestors of these Mongolian nomads might have conquered all of Europe. In A.D. 1240, while the cold of winter still gripped the European countryside, Batu, grandson of Chinggis Khan, moved his Mongol army west from its base on the south Russian steppes. Having already devastated and subjugated the Volga and Russian principalities with their superb horsemanship, brilliant cavalry tactics, and deadly accurate composite bows, the Mongols now set their sights on Central and Western Europe.

Batu divided his force into a center and two flanks. The northern flank crossed the frozen Vistula River and invaded Poland, Lithuania, and eastern Germany. It quickly defeated the Polish army, took Cracow, and then moved westward to defeat another army commanded by Duke Henry of Silesia at Liegnitz. The central force moved forward into Hungary under the command of Batu, while the southern flank swept through Transylvania into southern Hungary. In April 1241, the two flanks joined Batu and completely demolished a large army commanded by King Bela IV of Hungary at the Sajo River near Budapest, taking the town of Pest. After resting for a few months, Batu launched another campaign into Western Europe in December of 1241. Crossing the frozen Danube River, he sent scouting/raiding parties southwest into northern Italy and north toward Vienna while positioning his main force for the next series of battles.

Western Europe was spared this invasion when "pony express" riders brought Batu the news that the Mongol Emperor Ogedai had died in Mongolia on December 11, 1241. Mongolian law required that the descendants of Chinggis Khan return home to select the next emperor, so Batu, poised at the outskirts of Vienna, withdrew his troops to the southern Russian steppes and turned his attention to affairs of state in Mongolia. For reasons not clear, the Mongols never again moved westward, even after the succession was settled. Western Europe escaped unscathed.

The military might of these nomadic pastoralists from Inner Asia is one of the remarkable stories of human history. Batu was one of several descendants of Chinggis Khan whose armies swept over most of the Eurasian continent in the 13th and early 14th centuries and conquered all in their path including Russia, Persia, Afghanistan, Syria, Tibet, Korea, and the jewel of their empire—China. That a small, nomadic population of herders living in felt tents and riding horses the size of large ponies was able to burst out of Inner Asia and conquer so much of the known world is a tribute to the extraordinary military skill and administrative genius of Chinggis Khan and his immediate descendants.[1] It was also a function of the Mongols' way of life—their nomadic pastoralism.

1. By the mid-13th century, Mongol armies generally also included non-Mongol allies and conquered peoples such as the various Turkic tribes.

(opposite) The herders are excellent horsemen and love to ride. This young man asked us to take a photo of his horse and bring it back on our next trip.

Although the Altai Mountains look bleak and unproductive, Mongolian nomads have prospered here for centuries.

Nomadic pastoralism is one of the great advances in human cultural evolution. Scholars generally agree that it developed roughly 10,000-12,000 years ago at the same time as the start of agriculture, although some argue that it preceded farming. Like agriculture, it was a major improvement over the hunting and gathering way of life that hitherto had been universal.

In hunting and gathering societies, the human population exercises no control over the reproduction of the flora and fauna on which it depends. It moves in accordance with the natural rhythms of the plants and animals. Pastoralists also depend on animals and plants, but they dictate their movements and harvest their products, such as meat, milk, and skins, some of which they consume and some of which they barter. The success of the pastoral endeavor depends on ensuring a continual source of these products, i.e., keeping the animals healthy and reproducing.

To do this, herders move their animals to exploit the seasonal ebb and flow of vegetation and maximize the transfer of energy from vegetation to livestock. For pastoralists, therefore, mobility—nomadism—is inherent to their adaptation. Depending on the characteristics of the environment and the climate, some pastoralists move hundreds of miles, while others move only 5 to 10 miles at a time. Similarly, in some areas or during certain years, nomads may make 10, 20, or 30 such moves in a year, whereas in other areas they may move just a few times. But the way of life we have come to know as nomadic pastoralism—in the present and in the past—adheres to the pastoral imperative. Having assumed control over animals, the herders must decide how to use the natural cycle of vegetation growth to secure food for the livestock, and, in turn, themselves. Nomadic pastoralists, therefore, have to determine where to graze their livestock on a day-to-day basis and resolve when to move the entire camp to a new area.[2]

The mobility of the traditional way of life in Mongolia lent itself to warfare. Not tied to fields and irrigation works, and possessing riding horses and transport animals such as yaks and camels, people and their herds could easily move long distances without loss of productivity. Moving an army was in one sense an extension of moving a campsite, and fitting out a large cavalry force required very little in the way of special training, equipment, or animals. The main source of food—livestock— could accompany the army as long as there was vegetation along the march. The nomads were also experienced in riding and in the use of weapons. They hunted on horseback with bows and arrows, raided other tribes, and always had to be ready to defend their own herds against attacks. Moreover, their main weapon, the composite bow, was, for the 12th century, a "state-of-the-art" weapon.

---

2. Modern ranchers have adopted an alternative solution to this problem—they stay put but provide supplementary food for their animals.

Invented in Asia to be effectively shot from horseback, the composite bow allows the rider to turn easily in the saddle and shoot from either side while riding at full speed. Though it is short, it is extremely powerful. This power comes from its composite structure and its shape. Unlike European bows, which are long and made from a single piece of wood, the Mongolian composite bow is made of many pieces of horn and sinew glued onto a thin strip of wood. When unstrung, the ends curve away from the body. Stringing them involves pulling back these ends (toward the body) so that they stand up and down. This creates enormous test, giving the bows a range of up to several hundred meters.

In a world where weapons propelled by human muscle power were still dominant, the hard-riding, skilled archers of Mongolia were superbly preadapted for use as a mounted military force simply by being nomadic pastoralists. United under the leadership of Chinggis Khan and his descendants, they were forged into a formidable mounted juggernaut.

The Mongol Empire lasted for about 175 years, until the mid-14th century—a period roughly as long as from U.S. independence in 1776 to the Korean War in 1950. It then quickly faded from history. After Chinggis Khan's death, the empire divided into four Khanates ruled by his descendants. One was centered in China and Mongolia, a second in Iran, a third in Transoxiana, and the fourth, Batu's "Golden Horde" Khanate, in southern Russia. These Khanates gradually became politically and economically independent and assimilated into the less warlike cultures of the peoples they conquered. In the mid-14th century, the Mongol dynasties in Iran and China were deposed. In China this occurred in 1368 when native Chinese overthrew the Mongol Yuan Dynasty and forced the Mongols to withdraw to Mongolia. The Golden Horde lasted another century, but the Mongols never regained their grandeur.

In the Mongolian heartland, internal conflicts absorbed the decentralized Mongol tribes, leaving them vulnerable until they were subjugated by the Manchu rulers of China (the Qing Dynasty) at the end of the 17th century. Mongolia then became a part of the Manchu Empire.

For the next two centuries, pastoralism continued as the way of life in Mongolia, while a quasi-feudal society took root with nomad princes controlling fixed territories. At the same time, Mongolia came to be dominated by Chinese traders who monopolized business and money lending. The combination of an exploitive feudal elite and a predatory alien trading class resulted in stagnation and backwardness for much of the countryside.

Another round of political change in Mongol history began with the fall of the Manchu Dynasty in China in 1911. Mongolian leaders declared their independence from China and set up a new government under the rule of the Jetsundamba Hutuktu, the highest incarnate Lama of Mongolian Buddhism. The Bogdo Khan ("Holy Ruler"), as he was called, established an army and began to rule Mongolia as an independent state. China, however, resisted these moves, claiming Mongolia was still part of China, and in 1919 Chinese troops reoccupied the Mongol capital, then known as Urga.

Mongolians, however, were intent on freeing themselves from Chinese domination. A coalition of nationalists and communists drove out the Chinese in 1921 with the help of troops from the newly established Soviet Union. Three years later, the Mongol communists dispensed with their nationalist allies and established the Mongolian People's Republic, the second communist state in the world and the first in Asia.

For the next seven decades, the Mongolian People's Revolutionary Party (MPRP) ruled the country. It worked closely with the Soviet Union, which became Mongolia's main trading partner and primary source of political leadership and economic aid. Mongolia's internal political and economic development mirrored that of the U.S.S.R. in most ways, including a terrible Stalinist period complete with collectivization of nomads, purges, liquidations, and the destruction of religion. The communists destroyed more than 700 monasteries in the 1930s and killed thousands of monks.

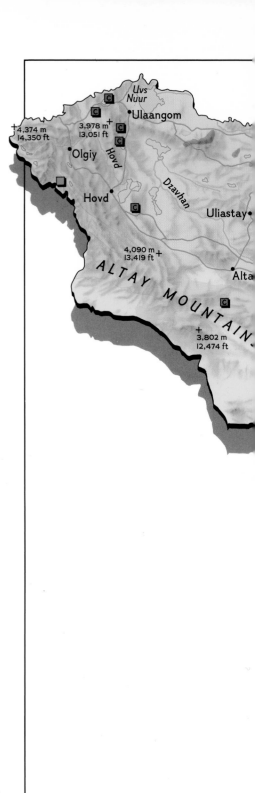

(previous pages) Winter winds at camps high in mountain valleys can howl at minus 20° to minus 50°F.

22

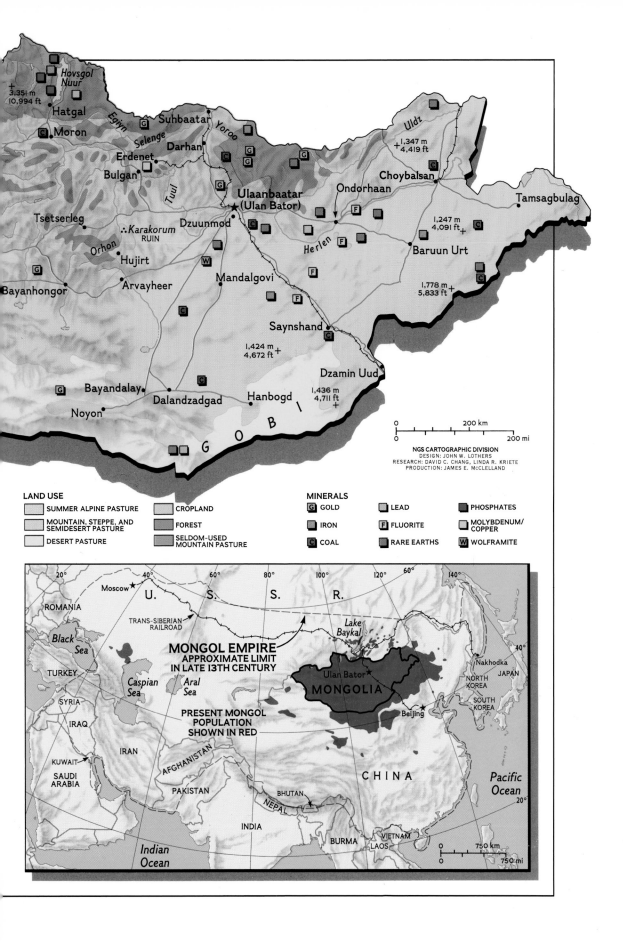

Hovsgol
Nuur
+3,351 m
10,994 ft
Hatgal
Egiyn
Selenge
Yoroo
Uldz
Suhbaatar
Moron
Darhan
Erdenet
Bulgan
Tuul
Ulaanbaatar
(Ulan Bator)
Ondorhaan
+1,347 m
4,419 ft
Choybalsan
Tamsagbulag
Tsetserleg
∴Karakorum
RUIN
Dzuunmod
Herlen
1,247 m
4,091 ft +
Baruun Urt
Orhon
Hujirt
Arvayheer
Mandalgovi
1,778 m
5,833 ft +
Bayanhongor
Saynshand
1,424 m
4,672 ft +
Dzamin Uud
1,436 m
4,711 ft +
Bayandalay
Dalandzadgad
Hanbogd
G O B I
Noyon

0	200 km
0	200 mi

NGS CARTOGRAPHIC DIVISION
DESIGN: JOHN W. LOTHERS
RESEARCH: DAVID C. CHANG, LINDA R. KRIETE
PRODUCTION: JAMES E. McCLELLAND

LAND USE

▢ SUMMER ALPINE PASTURE	▢ CROPLAND	
▢ MOUNTAIN, STEPPE, AND SEMIDESERT PASTURE	▢ FOREST	
▢ DESERT PASTURE	▢ SELDOM-USED MOUNTAIN PASTURE	

MINERALS

G GOLD	LEAD	▢ PHOSPHATES
IRON	F FLUORITE	▢ MOLYBDENUM/ COPPER
C COAL	RARE EARTHS	W WOLFRAMITE

20°   40°   60°   80°   100°   120°   60°   140°

Moscow ★

U. S. S. R.

ROMANIA

TRANS-SIBERIAN
RAILROAD

Lake
Baykal

Nakhodka

JAPAN

Black
Sea

TURKEY

MONGOL EMPIRE
APPROXIMATE LIMIT
IN LATE 13TH CENTURY

40°

Caspian
Sea

Aral
Sea

Ulan Bator ★

NORTH
KOREA

SYRIA

IRAQ

MONGOLIA

SOUTH
KOREA

KUWAIT

IRAN

**PRESENT MONGOL
POPULATION
SHOWN IN RED**

Beijing ★

SAUDI
ARABIA

AFGHANISTAN

PAKISTAN

C H I N A

Pacific
Ocean

20°

BHUTAN

NEPAL

INDIA

BURMA

VIETNAM

LAOS

Indian
Ocean

0	750 km
0	750 mi

Despite Mongolia's democratic revolution,
this poster of Lenin exhorting the masses
continued to have a prominent place in
downtown Ulaanbaatar through the
summer of 1993.

Electric trolley buses make commuting
around Ulaanbaatar easy.

The goal of the Mongolian Revolutionary Party was to transform Mongolia from an underdeveloped nation of herders into a modern agro-industrial "socialist" state. New urban industrial centers (mostly mining) were developed, and Mongolia went from a country that was 78% rural in 1956 to one that was 58% urban in 1989! The Mongolian communists had no use for old customs or nostalgia. Mongolians needed to know Marxism-Leninism, so Russian language study was made mandatory in school. This enabled many, if not most, of the country's intelligentsia to study and travel in the Soviet Union and East Europe; reciprocally, tens of thousands of Russians and East Europeans have lived and worked in urban Mongolia. Thus, while Mongolia's capital city, Ulaanbaatar—"Red Hero"—was 2,900 miles from Moscow, intellectually and emotionally it was right next door.

Mongolia's elite, therefore, were well informed about Gorbachev's reform policies in the U.S.S.R. and the spread of democracy in East Europe in the 1980s. The Mongolian equivalent of glasnost, *il tod* ("openness"), however, did not ease widespread discontent, and in December 1989 a series of large demonstrations in Ulaanbataar shook the Revolutionary Party into action.

At this crucial juncture in Mongolia's history, the MPRP agreed to implement a multiparty democracy. Free, internationally supervised elections were held successfully in July 1990, and a coalition government committed to transforming Mongolia into a market economy was installed a month later. Mongolia became the first Asian country to discard communism and embark on the difficult path of radical political and economic transformation.

It was our interest in these political transformations that brought us to the Altai Mountains. As professors of Social (Mel) and Physical (Cynthia) Anthropology at Case Western Reserve University in Cleveland, Ohio, we journeyed to Mongolia to study the society, economy, and biology of these descendents of Chinggis Khan after 70 years in a communist state and while they were beginning the exciting transition to a market economy and democratic government.

Our research plan was to concentrate on the back-country Mongols—the herders who still live in traditional felt *ger* ("yurts" as we call them, from the Russian word derived from a Turkish word), and like their ancestors, still herd sheep, goats, yak, camels, and horses. We wanted to live in their encampments, in *ger*, and study their way of life firsthand.

We arrived in Ulaanbaatar, Mongolia's capital, on September 1, 1990. Ulaanbaatar is a large city of 600,000, built in the drab concrete apartment-building style found all over Russia. However, when we first arrived, the atmosphere was anything but glum. Mongolia's first democratic election had just been held, and the Mongols were ecstatic. Even though the Revolutionary Party—the former communists—won the election easily, in the spirit of the new democracy it agreed to form a multiparty government. The air of optimism was contagious. At least a score of independent new newspapers were hawked on the capital's street corners, and Mongolians talked eagerly about the new parliament, the impending formulation of a constitution, and the future.

There was a feeling among Mongols that their country was now on the road to cultural revitalization and economic prosperity. For example, Academician Sodnam, an internationally known physicist and president of the Mongolian Academy of Sciences, was upbeat and eager for change. Discussing the significance of the democratic revolution for Mongolia's herders he said, "*Negdel* (herders' collectives) were a colossal mistake. Mongolia has the same number of livestock now as 50 years ago because this system didn't work. It stifled the nomads' initiative. Our new government has to eliminate them quickly. We need to return the animals to the nomads and let them operate as they did traditionally—under a free market economy." Only a few years ago such views could have landed a person in prison.

Everywhere we went people were outspoken, savoring the freedom of their new democracy, and we were told repeatedly that Mongolia's Soviet-style "command economy" had sapped the will of the people to work hard.

Ulaanbaatar ("Red Hero"), Mongolia's capital, contains one quarter of the country's population. It is an incongruous combination of concrete buildings and thousands of traditional ger *where many of the urbanites reside due to a shortage of apartments.*

The stylish Western dress of these shoppers on a downtown thoroughfare in Ulaanbaatar testifies to Mongolia's integration in the former Soviet bloc. Many of Mongolia's intelligentsia traveled and studied in the former U.S.S.R. and East Europe.

Aspiring to become the next "Asian Tiger," Mongolia initiated ambitious projects such as the construction of a luxurious tourist hotel in downtown Ulaanbaatar. Completion of the Chinggis Khan Hotel is now long overdue, owing to shortages of supplies and funds.

Academician Dzanchev, the very articulate director of the Academy of Sciences' Institute of Biology, shared this optimistic enthusiasm. Over dinner at a local restaurant he confidently told us, "Mongolia will be all right. We have a well-educated urban population with a high level of scientific sophistication. There will be a few hard years during the transition to markets, but I think that in a very short time Mongolia will become a new 'Asian Tiger.'"

But there was also the realization that Mongolia remained quite different from newly democratized Hungary and Poland. Altan Tuya, a young, very modishly dressed woman employed by Mongolia's new Chamber of Commerce, expressed this. "There are no models and theories about how to privatize a nomadic herding economy," she said. "We in Mongolia are moving into uncharted waters, and it will not be easy. We will have to learn as we go."

Hawkers selling the newspapers of dozens of new political parties (including a Buddhist party and a Green party) were a graphic expression of the new political freedoms experienced in Mongolia after it became the first Asian country to discard communism in 1990.

Despite the excitement in Ulaanbaatar, our aim was to learn what was going on in the countryside among the nomadic herders who were the backbone of Mongol society and economy. So, after two weeks in the capital, we flew to Hovd Province—840 miles west in the heart of the Altai Mountains. The four-hour flight in an old twin-engine Russian Illyushin gave us an unexpected glimpse of both the past and present—of the deeply ingrained inefficiency of the old communist system and the new freedoms of Mongolia's democracy.

The old ways were immediately clear. The flight was overbooked, and too many "open-seating" boarding passes had been distributed. People were pushing and shoving from all directions to climb the narrow, rickety boarding stairs. As take-off neared, those without seats weren't concerned—they simply squeezed in to sit as best they could between seats for take-off, and then became "standing room" passengers.

And as for the new ways, one literally hit us on our heads. While dozing during the long flight we were abruptly awakened by a sharp smack. Startled, we looked up and saw a rotund, smiling Buddhist monk going down the aisle blessing each passenger with a rap of his rosary. Like many other aspects of traditional Mongolian culture, Buddhism was making a comeback as Mongols actively sought to rediscover their pre-Marxist roots. The monk seemed a bit tipsy to us, but the other passengers accepted him with the good-natured exuberance that we came to appreciate as a Mongol characteristic.

After spending a day in the provincial capital (Hovd) meeting officials, we drove five hours in a jeep to the administrative center of Moost district. It is a small "town" consisting of 30-40 buildings and shops and scores of *ger* in which almost all of its 1,500 residents live. The government and collective officials briefed us and arranged for the local mail truck to take us to the herding encampment at Tsaganburgas, 18 miles to the west, to begin our work. Everything went perfectly until we were about to leave. Then a leading official casually ended his comments by advising, "Speak frankly and honestly with the herders and try not to do anything to anger them."

Internal communication in Mongolia, a huge country the size of Western Europe, was facilitated by inexpensive airline flights while Mongolia was still receiving Russian petroleum products and spare airplane parts. Twin-engine Illyushin planes plied the route between Ulaanbaatar and other provincial capitals such as Hovd before gasoline shortages in 1991-92 began to disrupt schedules.

Moost, the district center of our research site, is located in a broad valley within the heart of the Altai Mountains. It contains 30 or 40 one- and two-story buildings and apartments, but most of its 1,500 residents live in ger.

Developing rapport was essential to the success of our research, so we immediately asked him what we should be careful about. Mongols are straightforward and direct, and he replied, "Be careful about taking pictures. They do not like to have their photos taken."

We were aghast. We had planned to document their lifestyle with photographs and were carrying hundreds of rolls of film. The official went on to explain, "The national tourist agency, Zhuulchin, brings foreign hunters to this area to hunt the Marco Polo sheep (argali) and the ibex mountain goat. The local herders, however, are forbidden to hunt these and receive none of the hunting fees. They resent the foreign hunters, so when some hunters took photographs of them from their jeep, the nomads complained and demanded we send them away." Thus, something we had taken for granted now became our first major hurdle.

Luckily, when we explained to the nomads at Tsaganburgas and other camps why we wanted to take hundreds of candid photographs, they graciously agreed—although they were careful to tell us not to take "embarrassing" pictures, such as drunks or people relieving themselves in the fields. They are a proud people who want to be represented with dignity.

The trip to Tsaganburgas was uneventful until we encountered the herd of sheep mentioned earlier and stopped to get a better view of them. The older of the two horsemen rode over in a leisurely canter. A deeply suntanned man, apparently in his sixties, he dismounted agilely, greeting us with a big smile and a *"Sain bainu?"* ("How are you?"), *"Saixan namrijija bainu?"* ("Is your fall going well?").

As we were introducing ourselves and asking some questions, he pulled a thin, foot-long metal pipe from inside his right knee-high boot and filled its tiny bowl with half a teaspoon of tobacco. The old man was neither shy nor obsequious nor hostile. He exuded a pride and self-confidence that we would find inherent in the Mongol personality. He appeared to be thoroughly amused and completely nonplused to have met his first two Americans one day while out herding his sheep and goats. We imagined he would have quite a story to tell when he returned home.

His clothes combined modern and traditional styles. He wore a *del*, the knee-length Mongolian national gown that is fastened at the side and shoulder by several small buttons and bound by a wide sash of brightly colored silk wrapped several times around the waist. But he also wore Western-style tall black-leather boots and a white cloth cap that looked a lot like a yachting hat to us—although Mongolia is completely landlocked. Lighting his pipe with a match, he explained that he was a member of the same nomadic herding collective as the nomads at Tsaganburgas—our first destination—and that most of the sheep he was herding belonged to the *negdel* (collective) while a few belonged to his private herd.

At the the site of main district and negdel *offices, there is a constant stream of herders riding to town to conduct business. Most use horses, but a few come on two-humped Bactrian camels.*

After a few minutes he tapped the ash from his pipe and rose, saying with a smile, "You know, I heard on the radio that your Foreign Minister Baker has visited our capital, and that our two countries are now friends. That is good. Please come to visit my camp later. It's not far from Tsaganburgas. We can talk more then. I have many questions to ask you about America, and I have a lot to say about the situation here. A lot is changing."

Older nomads carry long metal pipes wrapped in brocade in their right boot. The tiny bowls hold only a pinch of tobacco and take as much time to fill and light as to smoke. Younger men prefer cigarettes.

Mounting effortlessly, he cantered off, his *dzaa, bayarta* ("good-bye") trailing off in the wind. As we watched, we hoped that the rest of the nomads would receive us as graciously.

They did, and this book is one result of that research. Cynthia and Mel visited this nomad community together for three months in the fall of 1990 and for two months in the spring of 1991. Mel made a third visit with graduate student Sherylyn Briller in the summer of 1992. During these visits we were fortunate to meet many hospitable and helpful nomads like the old herder and to make good friends. We learned the nomads' problems and aspirations, their values and prejudices, their strengths and weaknesses. We also came to like, admire, and respect these straightforward and proud pastoralists, feeling privileged to have been allowed by them to share a small part of their lives.

It is somewhat ironic that today's Mongols, like their ancestors who rode into Europe with Batu in the 13th century, are on the move and are again looking toward the West. This time, however, their intent is peaceful —not to conquer, but to shift from a rigid Marxist-Leninist totalitarian system to a Western-style democracy and market economy.

This book is their story—a chronicle of their nomadic pastoralism, the dramatic changes they experienced under 70 years of communism, and their adaptation to the enormous political and economic transformation that has engulfed their country.

Cold weather does not stop the nomads' work.

"NATURE IS OUR MANAGER"

BURGID DIED A SLOW DEATH ON THE COLDEST DAY OF WINTER IN 1990. Although he had lived all his 53 years in the Altai Mountains, he misjudged the weather that fateful day. He didn't know it, but the temperature was around -50°F, and gusting winds made the wind-chill factor even lower.

He set out early in the morning to round up horses grazing unattended in the mountains, and then drove them to water, but along the way the cold gradually sapped his strength. After dismounting to help water the herd, he found himself unable to remount due to advancing frostbite. He was miles from his camp, and must have known he was facing death. But he was a Mongol and did not give up. As the nomads reconstructed events, he walked toward his winter campsite as best he could, and when that became impossible, crawled until the icy wind finally sucked the last glimmer of warmth from his body. He almost made it—they found him the next day only a kilometer from his *ger*.

Winter comes quickly in the Altai Mountains. On this November day the temperature was already around 0°F.

The Moost nomads were well aware of the overwhelming and uncontrollable power of nature and their subservience to it. Haltarjav, an older, experienced herder, conveyed the essence of this one day in his terse reply to a question about his herd management strategy. After thinking for a moment or two, he replied succinctly, "Nature is our manager."

Nestled in the heart of Central Asia, the steppes and mountains of Mongolia are among the world's least hospitable environments—the cold there is awesome, the fury of nature an ever-present threat to survival. Yet for the remarkable nomads of Mongolia, these frozen wastelands have for centuries offered a homeland in which they have flourished.

Sandwiched between Siberia and China, Mongolia is a huge landlocked country of 604,100 square miles. It is physically larger than all of Western Europe, but its total population of 2.1 million is only the size of Budapest. Mongolia's landmass experiences a continental climate with low precipitation, long winters, and a preponderance of sunny days—there is sunshine 70% of the year. The average temperature (the midpoint between the daily high and low) is below freezing for seven months a year, and more than half of the country is underlaid with permafrost. The average elevation is 5,100 feet.

(below, left) Accumulated snow lingers in some narrow valleys through May and June.

Mongolia has a complex geography with four major zones. The famous Gobi Desert covers much of the southern part of the country. It is primarily an arid rangeland where camels, sheep, and goats can be maintained, but where it is difficult to herd cattle. To its east is a vast undulating expanse of grassland plains that extends for hundreds of miles to Mongolia's eastern border. Treeless and relatively flat, it is classic pastoral country. Mongolia also has two main mountainous regions. The Hangai in north central Mongolia is forested with deciduous and evergreen species, while the Altai Mountain Range in western Mongolia—the site of our research—is treeless and resembles Tibet. The Altai Range extends for hundreds of kilometers from Siberia to the Gobi and contains Mongolia's highest peak, Mt. Huyten Orgil at 14,350 feet.

These four geographic zones differ in many ways but share two basic features: each experiences Mongolia's extraordinarily bitter climate and each has extensive pastureland supporting tens of thousands of herders.

A herd moves to a bare area to graze, followed by herders on foot, collecting dung.

Treeless and rugged, the Altai Mountains project a stark majesty.

(below) Scraping snow from the roof of a ger prevents leaks when the heat of the stove melts the snow.

(above) In winter, the herders generally disperse,
camping either by themselves or in small clusters
together with a child or relative. (below and right)
Tethering yak calves overnight prevents suckling and
ensures that their mothers do not stray far.

The nomadic pastoralists of the Altai Mountains raise what Mongolians refer to as the "five kinds of animals"—sheep, goats, cattle (mostly yak), horses, and camels. In Moost, 61% of the livestock are sheep, 26% goats, 7% yaks, and 3% each are horses and camels. These animals provide the nomads' livelihood. One herder we knew explained this to us: "The animals are our food and money. They give us dairy products and meat to eat, dung to warm our *ger*, and wool and skins to make our felt and clothes. We look after the livestock well, and they give us what we need."

Although the nomads use virtually all parts of all the five kinds of livestock, sheep are the most valuable. In addition to wool and meat, sheep provide some milk and a critical resource—the skins with heavy fleece that are used for winter clothes. Yaks, on the other hand, are the main source of dairy products. Unlike sheep, which give milk for only a few months in summer, yaks give milk for almost the entire year, and just three or four lactating female yaks can provide a family of six all the milk, butter, and cheese it needs. Yaks also provide meat, hair, and skins for the herder's rawhide ropes and horse tack.

It is sometimes advantageous to use a winter campsite that has no running water. In such cases, herders freeze blocks of ice in November and transport them by camel to their winter campsites where they are melted as they need them. At such camps the animals are driven to a source of water every two days if there is no snow for them to eat and every third day if there is.

After a few weeks this stream will freeze solid and the herders will move to a new campsite.

Goats, like sheep, provide meat, milk, and skins for clothes. Their value has increased of late because they also provide cashmere, a fiber in demand on the international market. Cashmere is actually the undercoat of goats and is analogous to the soft undercoat we comb out of long-hair dogs, like collies, in summer. Yaks, horses, and camels also have this undercoat, but international law restricts the name "cashmere" to only the undercoat of goats, giving it much greater economic value.

Camels and horses are used mainly for transportation—camels to move camp and horses to ride. In the past—50 years ago—camels were rare in the Altai and yaks were the main beast of burden.

Climate drives the annual cycle of the nomad's life. During the four-month growing season from mid-May to mid-September, the mountain slopes and valleys are bright green and evenings are frost free. In fall, the growing season ends and the temperature begins to drop. The bitter cold of winter begins in earnest in November and continues through May when the cycle of new growth begins anew. The nomads' animals, therefore, survive on senescent vegetation for eight months of the year.

One old nomad's explanation of his herding practices highlighted the Mongols' basic herd management strategy. "Fat animals," he said, "survive the long winter better so we try to fatten our animals as much as possible during summer. If there is poor grass in summer the animals go into winter thin, and there is likely to be high mortality for all ages, particularly if the winter is harsh." We asked how often bad years occur, and he replied, "It seems we get hit every decade. For example, in 1984 we had a severe summer drought. At first we thought the rains were just late, but after the grass failed to grow well we drove a third of our herd north in the hopes of finding better pasture there. In the end, however, we were not very successful and lost many animals." According to the records we checked, Moost district actually lost 18% of its herd that winter. Figure 1 shows the annual fluctuation during the last 26 years.

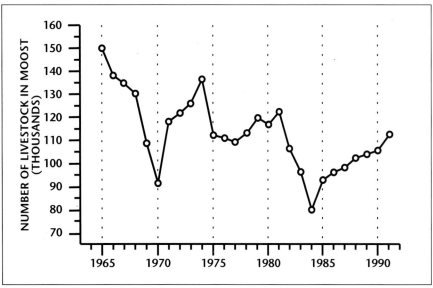

FIGURE 1

A nomad neighbor related his experience of how such disasters come about. "It can happen fast," he said. "If a heavy snow doesn't melt or if the snow starts to melt and then refreezes to form a layer of ice, the grass is covered and the animals can't eat." When we asked about the hay he cuts for winter use, he replied, "We cut grass in summer to use as fodder in such circumstances, but there is not enough to supplement grazing for the entire herd, so in a matter of days one can lose half or even all of his animals. With no food, the animals quickly succumb to the cold."

Usually strong winds drift the snow and expose some grass while the bright sun quickly melts the rest. But when all the vegetation is covered, the nomads are helpless.

We asked the old nomad to explain what he did to "put fat on" his herd and he laughed, amused by what must have seemed a naive question. "It all hinges on taking the animals to where the grass is best," he said. "Some herders are very concerned about their animals and really worry about this, but others are lazy and pay no attention. The good herders will move to better pastures as many as 15 or 20 times a year to give their animals the best possible food, while some poor herders move only a few times."

We found there are many reasons why and when the nomads move. They vary from year to year since the nomads are continuously micro-adapting to climatic conditions and the quality of available pasture. Sometimes they move because the grass near a campsite becomes exhausted and the herd's daily trips from the campsite expend too many calories in travel, and sometimes, for example in winter, they move to sites that are more sheltered from the wind. Other times, they move because a type of vegetation the animals like is available somewhere else. For example, yak are taken high into the mountains in winter because they thrive on a type of plant found on the upper slopes. Such moves often require splitting the herd and establishing a main and a satellite camp.

A teenage boy returns from a long day of herding.

Mongols of all ages are accustomed to long days in the saddle.

When the nomads experience a good summer and a mild winter, the capacity for rapid herd increase is enormous. Adult female sheep and goats give birth yearly and frequently twin. The female lambs and kids themselves give birth at the end of their second year. Thus, three or four mild winters in a row can easily result in a doubling of herd size.

Mongols take a stoic pride in what they feel is their special ability to cope with the bitter winter cold. It was not surprising, therefore, that Mongolian officials and colleagues in Ulaanbaatar frequently expressed concern about *our* ability to handle Mongolia's frigid climate. They wondered whether two urban American professors could live in *ger* in late fall when the temperature normally drops below minus 0 °F, and suggested tactfully that we stay in the heated hostel in the Moost district center and commute daily by jeep to the herding camps. However, our research design required us to live with the herders, so we resisted politely, responding that we had lived with nomads in Tibet for extended periods at 17,000 feet and had experienced temperatures of -35 °F. This information worked wonders because Mongols identify closely with Tibetans, even though contact between Tibet and Mongolia had been severed for seven decades due to

Yaks are amazing animals that can function well at altitudes of 17,000–18,000 feet and at temperatures of minus 40–50°F.

communism. If we could handle "Tuvt," as they call Tibet, they agreed we would be all right in the Altai Mountains.

Ironically, we, in turn, were concerned about our urban Mongolian assistants/translators' apparent lack of preparation for the cold they were going to experience in the mountains. We worried that they were underestimating the need for warm clothing and boots and at one point raised the issue tactfully with one of them. He immediately put us in our place, responding with a mixed air of incredulousness and disdain, "But I am Mongol. We know about the cold!" And he and the other Mongols did—they all showed up at the airport well equipped for the fieldwork. For Mongols, coping with the cold was an everyday event that didn't require a lot of talk and thought.

TO MOOST

Moost district comprises 10,100 square miles of twisting mountains and valleys, 99.9% of which is pasture land used by 115,000 head of livestock and about 4,000 people. Ranging from 7,800 to 11,000 feet above sea level, it is a stark landscape without trees or even shrubs. To an outsider it can seem devoid of habitation, but in reality the mountains and valleys contain scores of named campsites—neighborhoods—such as Tsaganburgas, Moxor, or Boorg, each occupied at a particular time of year, usually by the same households.

Our arrival in Tsaganburgas, a herding camp used for about a month in fall, generated a lot of excitement. We were the first Americans these nomads had ever met. Many herders wanted to talk with us, and after we set up our *ger*, Haltar, our neighbor, immediately invited us for some milk-tea and nomad "hospitality."

Haltar is a 44-year-old herder whose household included his wife Badam, his wife's widowed mother Otgon, and five children. We were seated on the tiny foot-high stools called *sandl* that look like kindergarten furniture and are found in the guest section of every *ger*—the left side away from the door. Haltar began by taking an elegant agate snuff bottle from its bright silk brocade pouch; he offered it to each of us in turn as tradition dictates. Fortunately, we didn't have to inhale the snuff—loosening the bright coral stopper and sniffing near the opening is acceptable.

Offering a laden hospitality bowl to guests is an important element of nomad hospitality.

Two friends greet each other with the traditional, right-handed exchange of snuff bottles. Custom requires opening the cap and sniffing, but not actually inhaling snuff.

Badam, meanwhile, set out the "hospitality bowl" each household prepares for guests, and then went about making Mongolian milk-tea for us.

Mongolians use a type of compressed tea leaf that is called "brick" tea in English because it is rock solid and roughly the shape of a brick. It is made in China and Russia from the poorest quality tea by wetting the leaves and pressing them into a mold. These tea bricks eliminate bulk and are convenient to transport and store. They are used throughout Mongolia and Tibet.

Preparing tea requires first chipping off tea flakes with a knife or hammer. After these leaves are boiled in water, milk (about 1 part to 10), butter, and salt are gradually added and blended by tossing ladlefuls in the air above the tea cauldron. The resultant beverage, *suteytsai* (milk-tea), is white and tasty, though strangely neither like milk nor tea. Mongolian nomads keep a warm pot of tea handy and drink bowlfuls throughout the day.

The hospitality bowl was piled high with all sorts of goodies—thick chunks of homemade cheeses, sugar cubes imported from the U.S.S.R., chocolate-covered candies from Ulaanbaatar, and the staple grain food— *bordzig*. This is a soft pastry made from rolled-out wheat dough that is deep-fried in lard or cooking oil. The nomads make hundreds of these at one time and eat them for early morning and midday meals together with milk-tea, meat, cheese, and other dairy products. In the evening, they have a cooked meal, usually a stew.

The Mongols use a type of tea known as "brick tea." Rock-hard and compressed into the shape of a brick, it has relatively little bulk and is easy to transport. Tea leaves must be chipped off the brick with a knife or hammer. Tea leaves are boiled for 5 to 10 minutes in a large cauldron.

Bordzig, *a pastry made from wheat dough, is eaten together with milk-tea and cheese in the morning and at midday. In the evening, cooked foods such as stews and noodle soups are prepared.*

Herders make dozens of bordzig *at once, rolling them into a variety of sizes and shapes. The* bordzig *keep for days in plastic bags.*

Bordzig *dough is deep-fried in mutton fat or vegetable oil.*

The Moost nomads slaughter sheep quickly by making an incision in the chest cavity and severing the aorta.

Haltar had just slaughtered a sheep, so he also set out a big metal basin filled with freshly boiled lungs, heart, stomach, intestines, liver, and the Mongol's favorite delicacy—pieces of solid fat. Mongolians, we quickly learned, love meat and fat, and in fact consider meat without fat unappetizing and inadequate. Once, when we were trying to buy meat in Moost town, a young man we knew brought us a leg of mutton but refused payment because he said the meat wasn't good quality. It was lean, and taking money would be like cheating us.

The most sensational of all the miscellaneous bits of information we passed on about the U.S. was a comment Mel made about fat to five or six nomads who had stopped by our *ger* one night after herding. One of them asked if Americans eat much meat, and Mel replied that they do but they cut off the fat. From the darkness of our candlelit *ger* a herder immediately called out, "What do Americans do with the fat that is cut off?" Mel's reply that it is thrown away prompted an audible gasp of shock throughout the tent!

After mixing roughly one liter of milk with eight liters of boiled tea, and adding a little butter and salt, white Mongolian suteytsai *(milk-tea) is aerated by ladling the tea high into the air and letting it fall back into the cauldron.*

In addition to the numerous visits to nomads' *ger*, we also attended several major ritual events such as the "hair-cutting" (*daixawax*) ceremony where we experienced Mongolian hospitality on a large scale.

Hair-cutting is a traditional nomad rite that has survived socialism. It marks the point at which a child is considered to have survived the dangers of infancy—in Moost this occurs at either three or five years of age. Before this, parents do not cut their child's hair. As a consequence, we had a difficult time telling little boys and girls apart because both sported pigtails tied with bright, fluffy bows.

The hair-cutting rite normally takes place in fall when the nomads are camped close to each other and the peak work period of summer milking and butter-making is over. Parents invite scores of relatives, neighbors, and friends, and their *ger* is jam-packed. Outside, the scene resembles a suburban party in the U.S., except that instead of shiny parked cars, dozens of elegant horses are tethered alongside a few colorful Czech and Russian motorcycles.

At the parties we attended, women were seated on the right side of the *ger* and males on the left, with the elderly of each sex sitting at the far end of their row in the back. The elderly men sat on a bed-couch at the back of the *ger*. Brightly painted wooden tables about two feet high were set up in a rectangle around the stove in the center of the *ger*. They were laden with a half dozen big metal hospitality bowls overflowing with food.

Childhood in the herding camps is pleasant and relaxed. Children are indulged by parents and siblings, and there is little work to do.

After snipping a small lock of hair from the honored child, or in this case, twins, each guest puts it into the blue silk bag and offers a present and a wish for good luck.

(opposite) Guests attend two five-year-olds' "hair-cutting" ceremony in September 1990, when the hospitality plates were overflowing with food. Less than a year later, many of the food items were unavailable.

The tent was full of gifts for the child who was having his (or her) hair cut—bricks of tea, boxes of sugar cubes, packets of biscuits, boots, money, and toys. We gave as our gifts a bright carpentry set from the U.S.S.R. and a dark-skinned doll from Cuba that we had incredibly been able to buy at the Moost store. Then we took seats among the nomads and exchanged snuff bottles with those nearby. All of this pleased the nomads, who enjoyed seeing Westerners following Mongolian traditions. A frequent criticism we heard about Russians was that they looked down on Mongolian customs.

As each guest arrived, the hosts served him/her a bowl of yogurt, a sip of a unique vodka locally distilled from milk (called *nirmalike*), and then tea. This was followed by an endless succession of meat, noodle soup, *bordzig*, and cheeses. The hair-cutting ceremony was a festive time that lasted all day. Guests talked and laughed, and spontaneous bursts of song filled the *ger* with haunting Mongolian folk melodies.

Full-scale nomad hospitality, whether at a celebration or just visiting someone's *ger*, involves serving milk-vodka and/or regular vodka. These are offered to each person in tiny porcelain shot glasses or small plastic bowls. The guest accepts the cup with the right hand outstretched and the left hand held under the elbow of the right, takes a sip, and passes it back to the server using the same gesture. The server tops it up and offers it to the next person.

Cutting the hair of the child-of-honor involved all of the guests. The child, or in one instance, twins, moved from guest to guest carrying a scissors and small bag. Each guest took the child onto his or her lap and snipped a small lock of hair with the scissors, stuffing the hair into the bag. The children we saw were extraordinarily well behaved about all this. Although a bit dazed by the mass of people and the commotion, they neither cried nor fussed, even when it was the turn of the foreign strangers to cut their hair.

"Hair-cutting" is a major event for a household, so the best food is served. Several of the household's fattest sheep are slaughtered, and the guests are served lots of meat.

Mongolia's sheep are known as "fat-tail" sheep because they have enormous tails that are mostly fat and can weigh 20 or more pounds. These tails were the centerpiece of the food display and were carved by the household head or an elder. The meat and fat were succulent, and if it hadn't been for our knowledge of the risks of high cholesterol we could have learned to enjoy eating the fat—although it is also possible that our recollection of its tastiness is somewhat colored by the endless sips of *nirmalike* and vodka we consumed.

Sharing the Mongolian diet brought home dramatically its unusually high content of animal fat. According to the World Health Organization, Mongolians consume a larger percent (88%) of their fat from animal products such as meat, milk, butter, cheese, and the *bordzig* pastries that are deep-fried in lard, than any other people in the world. However, when we discussed cholesterol levels with Nyamdorj, our anthropologist colleague at the Mongolian Academy of Sciences, we were surprised to learn that his data from a nomad district just north of Moost showed that the average cholesterol level was only 178 mg/dl (milligrams/deciliter), a level within the normal range in the U.S., where only levels above 200 mg/dl are considered cause for concern. We hope to make this puzzle the subject of a new study in the future.

A wooden paddle is used to churn butter from a yogurt mixture fermenting in a large leather or canvas bag hung on the ger wall.

The fat tail of the Mongolian breed of sheep has a place of honor at parties and is carved by the head of the household or an older male.

After removing the butter, the remaining milk is boiled in a big pot capped by a distilling cone. Arool cheese is formed in the pot and milk-vodka (nirmalike) in the cone.

The nomads' milk-vodka (*nirmalike*) is an ingenious byproduct of the milk-conversion process. Dairy products made from the milk of yak, sheep, and goats are major staples in the nomad's diet, but are produced mainly in summer when all the animals are lactating. Since milk spoils quickly, the Mongols have developed an effective process that converts the abundant summer milk into more easily storable products for later consumption.

The process entails making yogurt, then butter, and then cheese and *nirmalike*. Fresh milk is boiled and set aside in a container with a "starter" yogurt. After a day or two, the yogurt is transferred to a 16 gallon skin or canvas bag called a *huhur* that hangs on the inside left wall of every *ger*. This is done daily in summer and weekly at other times, depending on the amount of available milk. Butter is made by plunging a long wooden paddle up and down in the *huhur* to churn the yogurt mixture. The butter is removed and sewn into an airtight sheep stomach, where it keeps for up to a year.

The next day, the remaining liquid, the "buttermilk," is ladled into a huge wok-like metal cauldron and boiled. A three- to four-foot-high wooden distilling cone sits on the rim of the pot and is capped by a saucer filled with cold water. The steam from the boiling buttermilk rises in the cone, condenses on the saucer, and drips into a small pot hanging in the cone. This *nirmalike* is a clear liquor that is 10-12% alcohol. We especially enjoyed the *nirmalike* because it was relatively weak and allowed us to accept the nomads' hospitality without getting excessively drunk. Inebriation was not uncommon at celebrations, and drunk riding was definitely a hazard as party-goers headed home singing loudly, half in and half out of the saddle.

A cup suspended in the distilling cone catches the condensing droplets of nirmalike.

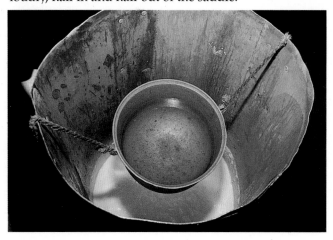

The tart cheese curds that coalesce during this boiling are drained, pressed into two-pound square blocks, and sun dried on the roof of the *ger*. This *arool* cheese is enjoyed year-round, but is especially important in the winter and spring when there is little or no fresh milk. One nomad we camped beside told us his household of seven people normally prepared 110-120 pounds of this cheese in summer and fall for use in winter, along with 45 pounds of butter and 100 pounds of another kind of cheese, called *bislik*, that is made without removing the butterfat.

Cream is another dairy delicacy. Yak milk, especially that of females with two-year-old calves, is high in butterfat. Boiled and left overnight, the cream rises to the top of the pan and semi-solidifies. This layer of sweet cream is lifted off, placed in a bowl, and eaten straight or spread on *bordzig* pastries. Alternatively, the cream may be ladled into a sheep stomach and enjoyed months later as "white cheese."

Winter preparations also often include preparing and transporting water and milk. It is common for herders to freeze blocks of milk and water in late fall and transport these to their winter site by camel. One nomad camped by a river at his fall site explained, "I will stay here until the river freezes, then I'll move to my winter campsite eight miles from here. It is not near water, but it has good grass and is well sheltered from the wind. So I freeze water here in pails and transport it in sacks to my winter camp where I bury it until I need to use it. It will take my six camels five trips [camels can carry loads of 600 to 900 pounds and can travel 30 miles a day]." When asked how his sheep and goats manage without water, he nodded and replied, "That is no problem. If there is no snow to eat, I drive them to a spring every other day, but if there is snow, I take them every third day." And then as afterthought he added, "Actually, even if I brought fresh water into my *ger*, it would freeze solid overnight, so transporting ice blocks by camel is the same as having a source of water nearby."

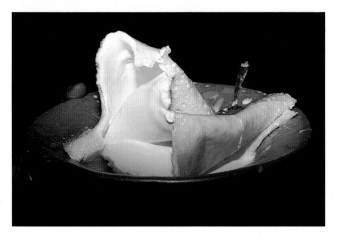

(top) Tart, arool *cheese being pressed into a two-pound square block. It is then dried and stored for use in winter and spring when fresh milk is scarce. (above) The layer of cream that rises to the top of yak milk is a special treat.*

Butter stays fresh for nearly a year when sewn tightly into a sheep's stomach.

Yaks give milk 10 months of the year and are the herder's main source of milk and dairy products. Four or five yaks can meet the milk needs of an average-size household.

While visiting our neighbor Haltar's *ger* in Tsaganburgas, we asked him about herding, the collective (*negdel*), and the political changes that were going on.

We had already heard from Puravdorj, the local district chief, that despite the prevalent Ulaanbaatar view that herders' collectives were a disaster and should be abandoned, here in the countryside the nomads did not wish to see their quick demise.

Puravdorj was an interesting amalgam of the best of the old and new. He was not some urban official unwillingly sent "down" to the countryside, but a local nomad from the next district who had done well in school and had moved up the ladder, serving as the Moost school principal for some years before becoming district head. He knew the life and attitudes of the herdsmen and was wonderfully at ease sitting in their *ger* drinking milk-tea and *nirmalike* and talking about their problems and hopes. He was a long-time Revolutionary Party member and the district's representative to the new national parliament called the Great Hural, but he was also now committed to democracy, the new market-economy reforms, and a better Mongolia.

When we asked what the nomads thought about collective versus market economics, Puravdorj answered frankly, shaking his head. "It varies, but in general they don't understand market economics very well and are afraid it will harm their income and threaten their welfare benefits. All they know is the *negdel* (the herding collective). It will take time to educate them about managing and marketing on a household basis. But it must happen. The Soviet Union can't help us anymore, and a free-market economy and trade with democracies like the U.S. and Japan is our only hope for security and prosperity." For the three months we lived with the herders in 1990, Puravdorj, now a democratically *elected* district head, traveled through the district in his small Russian jeep, meeting and talking with nomads—his constituents—in a manner surprisingly reminiscent of an American politician. In the past, the *negdel* chairman was also the district head, but the reforms of 1990 changed that, making the district head a separate elected official who was now the key rural administrative officer.

Mongolians are renowned for "airak," a slightly alcholic beverage from fermented mares' milk. In Moost, however, this was not common and only a few families milked mares. The horse milking season lasts about 30 days, when the grass is good. Mares are milked every two hours starting at 10 a.m. and ending at 8 p.m.

We were surprised by Puravdorj's comments, since we had heard so many negative opinions about the collective system in Ulaanbaatar, and about "command economies" in general. But sure enough, in our first lengthy conversation with a nomad, Haltar conveyed the ambivalence Puravdorj alluded to in response to our queries about collective and market economies. "I think the *negdel* has been good for us," he said. "We have plenty of food, free health care for our children, and free education. Two of my sons are in school at the district and my oldest daughter is in teacher's college in another province. But I am a Mongol, so if the government now says we need to change to have a better life, perhaps we do. At first we nomads vehemently hated the collectives and opposed their creation, but it turned out all right, so maybe going back to privatization and a market economy will also be good."

As Haltar indicated, the collective had a checkered history in Mongolia. In 1927, three years after the founding of the Mongolia People's Republic, the new communist government tried to force collectivization on Mongolia's nomads just as Stalin was doing to farmers in Russia. For the next few years, independent herders throughout Mongolia were ordered to give their animals to newly created collectives. Angry nomads responded by killing millions of head of livestock rather than turn them over. So terrible was the destruction that the government had to stop the program, and many in Mongolia like Academician Sodnam today believe that the nation has still not attained the number of animals it possessed before that slaughter.

In the 1950s, the communists again launched a collectivization campaign, this time using more indirect methods. *Negdel* membership was voluntary, but progressively heavier taxes on private herds forced the nomads to join—or go bankrupt. Within a decade, Mongolia was completely collectivized. The Moost *negdel*, called *Tuya* or "Light," exemplifies this. It began in 1951 with only 11 herders and 59 animals. By 1959 it had incorporated all the herders in the area and all but a few private animals that households were allowed to keep for their own consumption. In 1965, the first year for which we found local records of herd size, the *negdel* owned 85% of Moost's 145,000 head of livestock, a scant 15% being held privately by the herders' households.

Haltar continued his comments on the proposed change: "To be honest, I don't understand how a market economy will work. I've never sold my livestock products privately and don't know where I would do this. Who would buy my cashmere? We can't go to America to sell it. It's hard to envision how we could manage without the *negdel*." We asked him how the *negdel* helps him, and he smiled and replied with a twinkle in his eye, "Okay, I have much to tell you. But first eat some mutton."

(following pages) Seventy-eight years old, but still herding livestock on camel, this spry herdswoman did not see anything unusual about her herding on a cold day in May.

Although the Moost nomads never all congregate in one encampment, in some seasons dozens of white ger *converge along the banks of meandering streams for two or three weeks at a stretch.*

GER, HORSES, AND LAMAS

WE CAMPED AT TSAGANBURGAS FOR THREE WONDERFUL WEEKS. THE weather was sunny and mild, the nomads relaxed and leisurely, and the landscape stunning. Both sides of the clear blue stream that bisected the steep mountain valley were dotted with bright white *ger* and a colorful mix of sheep, goats, yak, and horses. Living there gave us our first insight into the simple but effective technology the nomads have developed over the centuries to cope with their harsh environment and to conduct their nomadic pastoralism.

Transportable shelters are essential to a pastoral nomadic way of life and, in the frigid cold of Mongolia, are a matter of survival, not just comfort. The Mongolian *ger*, as we happily found out by living in one, is superbly adapted to this. It is easy to put up, take down, and transport, and is also very warm and windproof. Nomad families can break camp and load all their possessions onto camels in roughly an hour.

It takes two people to tighten ropes to secure the heavy camel loads.

(opposite) A young woman contemplates where to pitch her ger at a new campsite.

(below) This camel train belongs to a pensioner who herds actively for three seasons and then moves to the more sheltered district center for the winter, leaving his livestock with younger relatives in the countryside.

A modular structure is the key to its effectiveness. The "wall" consists of four or five wooden, collapsible accordian-like lattice fences resembling those Americans use to prevent children from falling down stairs. Spread open and lashed together, they form a sturdy circular wall about five feet high. When it is time to move on, each section collapses compactly into a flat unit about three feet wide that is easily loaded onto a camel.

The roof section is also readily portable since it consists of 40 to 50

The Mongolian ger *is easily erected, dismantled, and transported. The wall consists of four or five accordion-like sections of wood lattices lashed together in a circle.*

detachable broomstick-like wooden poles about five to six feet long. One end of the pole fits into peg holes in the wooden "wheel" in the center of the roof that forms the opening for light and chimney pipes. The lower end is threaded with a rawhide thong that loops around a lattice crosspiece in the wall section. With these roof struts in place, the *ger* has a rigid, self-supporting frame, although large *ger* usually have an internal wooden pillar or two for additional stability. Most *ger* we saw were about 16 feet in diameter and 7½ feet high at the center.

Insulation and wind protection come from one or two layers of felt sections that are about 15 feet long and four to five feet wide. These are strapped onto the wall lattice and the roof and topped by sheets of white canvas, tied tightly with straps that circle the ger like ribbons on a huge birthday gift. When the herders fire up their metal, yak-dung stoves, the temperature inside the *ger* becomes quite comfortable. We could sit five to six feet from the fire without a coat when the temperature outside was in the low teens (fahrenheit). And after the fire died out at bedtime, the temperature inside the tent remained 15-20 degrees warmer than outside. But we could never forget the cold; when the outside evening temperature fell below 0 °F, the inside temperature dropped well below 32 °F and froze our water and meat each night.

Because the nomads of Moost live in a climate where there is only one growing season a year, they do not make long migrations to new pastures. The longest move we heard of took two days and was only 50 or 60 miles. Most were less, taking only a day. In Moost there is no advantage to moving hundreds of miles, since the seasonal pattern of grass growth is the same for hundreds of miles in every direction. When the grass ceases to grow in Moost in September, it does so throughout Mongolia and neighboring China. Livestock, therefore, subsist on standing vegetation for eight months of the year. The basic pasture migration strategy in Moost, therefore, is to leave enough standing vegetation (pasture) at the end of the growing season in September to suffice until the new growth appears the following May.

The ger *roof consists of 40 to 50 thin poles (12 per lattice section) attached to the wall by rawhide loops and stabilized by fitting into notches in a circular wooden "keystone" at the top of the tent.*

A first layer of white canvas over the frame brightens the inside of the ger. After securing the inner layer, one or two layers of felt pading is added to provide insulation for the bitterly cold months when the temperature dips to minus 30–50°F. A final layer of white canvas adds extra wind- and waterproofing.

Hunters bury metal traps at tunnel entrances to capture marmots, valuable for pelts and meat.

Twirling a tuft of yak-tail will arouse the marmot's curiosity. When it rises up to get a better look, the hunter has a chance for a good shot.

(opposite) Young men enjoy the challenge and prestige of breaking and rebreaking horses.

Of the five kinds of animals raised in Mongolia, the horse has the least economic value, but is clearly the most prized. It was easy to see why Mongols made such outstanding mounted warriors, for the nomads even today are superlative equestrians. A 13th-century assessment by a Chinese historian named Zhao Xung echoes this: "The Mongols are born in the saddle and grow up on horseback; they learn to fight by themselves as they spend all their life hunting the year-round." In many ways this is still true.

Hunting is very popular with men, although nowadays it is done with .22 caliber rifles and traps rather than bows and spears. Wolves and marmots are the main targets, since the government reserves other traditional human prey such as mountain goats and Marco Polo sheep for foreign sports hunters, but foxes and rabbits are also sought. Marmot hunting, in fact, is an important activity in Moost where roughly 5,000-10,000 pelts are harvested yearly during a fall hunting season. Marmot meat is considered a special treat of fall and is eagerly consumed, while the pelts are sold for manufacture into winter hats.

Men, women, and children all love to ride, and it was not unusual to see seven-year-old boys and girls herding on horseback. The Mongols, in fact, do not walk much. Moost households on the average owned nine horses and kept at least one mount saddled and tethered beside their *ger* during the day—like the family car in the U.S.—instantly available for herding, errands, or visiting. The rest of their horse herd grazed unattended in the mountains until their turn to serve. The riding horses are rotated every week or two since the horses "on duty" had less opportunity to graze than normal and lost strength quickly.

We learned that shooting a wolf is prestigious when we noticed one running across the road while driving to the provincial capital. The driver immediately swerved off the dirt road, pursuing it cross country. Yelling for us to hand him his rifle, which he kept behind the rear seat, he shot it from his open front door while careening wildly. In addition to the prestige of having killed a wolf, wolf meat is highly prized for its medicinal value and the pelt brings a good price. The district also pays a bounty to the hunter.

Bringing the main herd back to camp to select one or two as the new riding horses was always a lively occasion because most of the horses in the herd had not been ridden for months and were often semi-wild, racing back and forth to avoid being lassoed. We first saw this roundup in mid-October at the third encampment we visited—Moxorix, a yak encampment tucked high in the mountains at 9,500 feet beside a tiny stream that was already freezing over at night.

We were visiting with Ajii and his wife Shuraa when the camp suddenly filled with shouts and cries. A neighbor hurriedly opened Ajii's door and told him, "Come on, the horses are arriving." Ajii leaped up, grabbing his handmade rawhide lariat, and told us to come along also since we were about to see something "interesting."

Outside, two riders were racing back and forth trying to contain about 50 horses in a bunch against a steep rocky hill. Others in the camp now pitched in—on foot and horseback—to prevent the milling horses from breaking out of the pack. As several men started lassoing, it looked like a scene from the American wild west, with lassos flying and horses scattering. Eventually the right mounts were roped, and the owners very carefully inched forward hand over hand on the rope toward the horse to attach a halter. The other horses were set loose to graze in the mountains until new mounts were again needed. But the excitement was far from over. These horses had been running free in the mountains and were not enthusiastic about being saddled and ridden. So the best riders among the younger men in the camp got the job of re-breaking the horses for riding. The riders and watchers both enjoyed this "bronco busting" immensely.

(below) A horse herd is contained near a rock wall so that the men can identify and lasso the mount they want.

(opposite) Having lassoed his new mount, a herder cautiously attaches a halter.

Despite the rural, "cowboy" image, all the younger nomads had attended school for six or eight years and could read the national newspaper. Nearly everyone listened to the radio, and many were quite interested in the outside world, particularly with life in the U.S. Their government's abrupt switch from criticizing America and the evils of capitalism to extolling America's virtues had made them curious and somewhat puzzled. Haltar, our neighbor in Tsaganburgas, for example, surprised us the first day we interviewed him by suddenly asking, "Would it be all right now to ask *you* some questions?"

Adeptly rolling a cigarette from a torn piece of newspaper—a local custom one nomad joked about, saying, "Unlike the capital, here we don't read newspapers, we smoke them"—Haltar proceeded to rattle off a string of questions about America. Were there collectives? How much milk do sheep, goats, and cattle give, and do herders have to pay to go to school? When we explained that all farms and herds were privately owned, he thought for awhile and then asked, "Then who pays their pensions, and who sells their wool, meat, and milk?"

Surprised to hear this mention of pensions, we asked if rural Mongolians such as his 73-year-old mother-in-law received them. Haltar smiled, nodding, and told us with obvious pride in the *negdel* system, "Oh yes. Male herders get pensions at 60 years of age; females at 50 or 55."

This was one of many unexpected aspects about the life of these people. Visually, the herding camp looked like drawings and photos from the early 20th century. The herders lived in *ger*, burned dung, rode horses to herd their livestock, and wore the traditional Mongolian *del*. On a day-to-day basis, herders like Haltar were "traditional" nomadic pastoralists moving with their herds and harvesting their products. However, they enjoyed an amazing range of benefits from the socialist state and had also internalized a number of "socialist" ideas and values through a system of compulsory universal education.

(top) Some herders shoe their most valuable horses but most find it too expensive and forego shoes.

(above) Two-year-old male horses are generally castrated to keep them from becoming too rambunctious.

The nomads' horse herds often spend months grazing unattended high in the mountains, so when a horse is brought to camp for riding, it is semi-wild and has to be re-broken.

Cynthia got a firsthand example of this several weeks after we arrived when she gave a talk about the American education system to teachers at the district boarding school in Moost. During the question and answer period, a middle-aged teacher asked, "Is it true that when poor people die in America they are simply left on the streets to rot?" She was told later that this had been a standard propaganda example used in the schools.

And a few weeks later, a very smart and sympathetic *negdel* official asked Mel, "Could you comment a little on the condition of American Indians in the U.S.?" He had heard stories about the plight of Native Americans and wanted to know if it they were accurate. The nomads had been taught that capitalist society does not care about the poor and the weak, and they asked about this on many occasions. The principle of helping the poor and downtrodden had been deeply ingrained in them by the state, and we found it revealing that the transition to a market society was frequently described by the government as a change to a "humane" Mongolian brand of capitalism and market economy.

These questions about America, however, reflected more curiosity than hostility. In fact, during our first weeks in Tsaganburgas, we were often moved when everyday nomads offered *nirmalike* toasts to President Bush and the new friendship between America and Mongolia. We quickly came to like and admire these tough and down-to-earth nomads.

The democratization of Mongolia in 1990 was not simply a change in political and economic ideologies; it also entailed a shift in cultural attitudes. Mongolia's communist leaders had sought to create a new culture in Mongolia that in many ways was more socialist than Mongol. In the process, many traditional aspects of Mongol culture such as Buddhism and shamanism were prohibited and proclaimed as exploitive and superstitious. Democratization changed all that, and Buddhism, the dominant religion until its elimination in the 1930s, was making a comeback. Similarly, other traditional customs, such as the old Uighur writing script that had been replaced by the Cyrillic (Russian) alphabet were also being resurrected. In fact, Mongolia's national identity was being reevaluated. We saw a surprising TV show in Ulaanbaatar called, "Little Europe in Asia," that asked viewers to ponder whether Mongolians are Asians or Europeans. Many urban Mongols, we learned, feel much greater affinity with Europe (at least the part that had been socialist Europe) than the rest of Asia.

The resurgence of Buddhism was impressive. Mongols adopted the "Yellow Hat" sect of Tibetan Buddhism after Sonam Gyatso, the Tibetan head of that sect, traveled to Mongolia and converted Altyn Khan. The great khan then reciprocated and conferred the title "Dalai Lama" on Sonam Gyatso in 1578—*dalai* means "ocean" in Mongolian, and the title is generally taken to mean "lama whose wisdom or knowledge is as vast as the ocean."

Part of the summer religious "offering" ritual involves erecting prayer flags whose message is carried by the wind to the gods.

This title was applied posthumously to the lama's two predecessors, so Sonam Gyatso became the Third Dalai Lama. This relationship was solidified when a Mongol child was discovered as the Fourth Dalai Lama. The result of this was that the Yellow Hat sect gradually spread throughout Mongolia in the 17th century, and at the time of the Mongolian Revolution of 1921 there were roughly 580 monasteries and temples and 110,000 monks in Mongolia. Monks made up about one-third of the total population, although not all were celibate.

However, in the 1930s, monasteries were forcibly closed and the monks disbanded or killed. Buddhism in Moost, like the rest of Mongolia, was totally uprooted. The extent of this eradication was poignantly illustrated one afternoon when we asked a 73-year-old Mongol named Bayanzir if he were a Buddhist. The question took him by surprise, and he paused a few moments before responding. Stroking his chin absentmindedly, he finally said, "Well, when I was a child my parents were Buddhists. But in between there was no religion. Now Buddhism is once again allowed, but I don' t know anything about it so I don't really think I am a Buddhist." Bayanzir paused again, and then added, "But I think if monks come here to teach, I'll probably learn a little and again become one."

Worshippers, both herders and officials, arrived on horses and motorcycles to participate in an early summer ritual ceremony to propitiate Buddhist gods. The demise of communism has led to a resurgence of Tibetan Buddhism, the traditional religion of Mongolia. This ceremony was resumed in 1990 after a lapse of 50 years. Here the herders circumambulate a sacred cairn of stones in a clockwise direction, resuming a ritual practiced by their parents and grandparents.

The absence of private religion in Moost was striking during our 1990 visit. We encountered no elderly nomads using Buddhist prayer beads and just a few of the more than 50 *ger* we visited exhibited any religious paraphernalia. None had altars. Traditionally, the center rear of the tent (facing the door) had an altar with images of Buddhas and lamas, prayer books, and votive butter lamps. In 1990 this space was occupied by mirrors and collages of family photographs—socialist-approved secular substitutes for religious icons.

But religion had already begun a comeback at the time of our first visit. For the first time in decades, the traditional Buddhist "mountain-god offering" ceremony had been held in each of the *negdel*'s sub-ùnits, officiated by two old former monks from a nearby district who had resumed wearing monk's robes. Unlike the old days when this was a male affair, both men and women attended. However, bad weather and epidemics in several parts of the country led the newly emerging Buddhist leadership to declare that allowing women at the offering angered the gods and brought bad luck, so in 1991, tradition was adhered to and only men attended.

Mel joined the 1991 ceremony together with representatives from virtually every family in the sub-unit and the *negdel* chairman. It was typical of Buddhist mountain-god offerings in Tibet, in that it involved prayers read by monks,[1] circumambulation of stone piles (cairns) that supported prayer flags, and throwing food (cheese and yogurt) into the air as offerings to the gods.

Most of the men did not know what to do and closely followed the instructions given by the monks' lay assistant, who told people when to sit, to stand, and to circumambulate. Moreover, while some of the older nomads took the ceremony very seriously, some younger ones seemed a bit uncomfortable, joking and making fun of it. But the ritual took place without a hitch and represented a step in the return of institutionalized Buddhism.

By Mel's 1992 visit, things had gone further. Several nomads displayed photographs of incarnate lamas in their *ger*, and a few older nomads owned prayer beads and were saying prayers. The nomads now not only had to decide about capitalism and market economics, but also about religion, reincarnation, and monasticism.

1. The prayers were from Tibetan-language texts that the monks could read, but could not understand.

Buddhist monks, or lam, *as they are called in Mongolia, were banned in the 1930s (except for a few show monks in a temple in the capital). Here, two elderly* lam *from a nearby district preside over the rite, reading prayers in Tibetan, the language of Mongolian Buddhism.*

THE *NEGDEL*

AT FIRST GLANCE, NOMADIC PASTORALISM AND MARXIST-LENINIST SOCIALISM seem totally antithetical. The nomadic pastoral household represented freedom and autonomy, whereas the socialist command economy was characterized by rigidity and central control. Yet, in Mongolia, they were surprisingly compatible.

The heart of *socialist* pastoralism was the *negdel* or "herders' collective." These collectively organized enterprises were created to transform nomad society from a household-based pastoral economy to a Marxist-based communal one. Traditionally, each household controlled all of its herding, production, and marketing decisions, and owned the means of production—the livestock. Pastures were controlled by feudal lords but open to all herders.

Under socialism, the *negdel* owned the livestock and pasture-land and managed production. This arrangement eliminated large discrepancies in herd size and wealth, since the *negdel* was able to assign roughly analogous numbers of animals to households and pay salaries that didn't vary much. But as will be discussed later, it was far less successful in fostering high productivity.

Moost's *negdel* illustrates the general organization. It was run by a General Committee headed by a chairman who was inevitably a member of the Revolutionary Party. Beneath the committee were a few offices dealing with accounting and personnel, and then some small enterprises like a butter-making plant and the massive animal husbandry operation.

The *negdel*'s animals and herders were divided into five administrative sub-units called *brigad* ("brigades," from the Russian). Each of these had its own chief, appointed by the General Committee, and several employees such as an accountant and an animal specialist (zootechnician). Each *brigad* also had its own pastureland and "seasonal" administrative centers, one for summer and fall, and one for winter and spring.

Officially, smaller economic units beneath the *brigad*, called *soor*, consisted of several cooperating herding households, but in Moost these existed only on paper.

The del *is the national dress of Mongolia. It is fastened at the waist by a wide sash of bright colored silk or satin, and by buttons on the upper right-hand shoulder. The figure in the photograph is Altyngiril, the* negdel *chairman.*

(following pages) Because herds graze on natural vegetation, the rhythm of life is set by the daily movement of livestock into and out of camp.

The *negdel* (and *brigad*'s) land was divided into named pastures in accordance with traditional customs. There were no fences around the patures, but everyone knew the boundaries. The *negdel* (via the *brigad*) allocated seasonal pasture areas to every herder's household on the basis of herd size and composition. A number of households in a *brigad* were given rights to use the same area. Each was free to set up camp wherever they wanted within their assigned area, although the *negdel* determined when moves to winter, spring, summer, and fall pastures could commence. Herders tended to return to the same campsites year after year, and encampments frequently consisted of several closely related households. *Negdel* members were free to graze their private animals on the *negdel*'s pastures.

No private ownership of pastureland was known before the *negdel* began, so collectivization in a sense continued the traditional system of an open range within the group, the groups now being *negdel* instead of larger feudal territories. Moreover, since Moost traditionally was not a region where long winter migrations were made to avoid areas of heavy snowfall, these smaller territorial boundaries did not represent a radical break with tradition.

Roping a several-hundred-pound yak is just the first step in weighing it.

At the annual summer roundup, young men show their courage and skill by wrestling yaks into the weighing chute.

The *negdel* was not a corporation in the sense of members owning shares and receiving income based on these shares. Instead, member's income came from work performed under the management of the collective's leaders. Nevertheless, the herders had a say in deciding certain kinds of work policies through the mechanism of periodic meetings that brought together the leadership of the *negdel* and a representative from each member household.

In 1990, we attended such a meeting and were surprised at how heated some of the discussions were. In one instance, a group of nomads was agitated about the *negdel's* new policy of keeping a number of households with milk yaks near the district headquarters in winter so that its residents would have a readily available source of milk. The herders felt the yaks would be healthier if they were higher in the mountains, where the pastures were more suitable (as was traditionally done), and argued vociferously in favor of this even though moving to the higher campsites would mean they would have to live in harsher conditions. They succeeded in overturning the decision. Haltar, our neighbor from Tsaganburgas, was among them. He returned from the meeting that night, and the next day broke camp and left without a trace. The mobility of nomadic pastoralists is remarkable.

In early summer, yak, sheep, and goats are weighed before they are driven to Siberia to be sold as meat. A young man wrestles a yak into a stone chute that leads to an enormous scale.

(above) The negdel weighed sheep in the fall to determine whether production targets were achieved. Tin bath tubs atop heavy-duty scales made the job easy.

(opposite) Animals are corraled for counting and weighing.

Sheep and goats are weighed by driving them into a chute atop a scale set up in front of collective officials who record the animal's and owner's information.

But for more far-reaching administrative issues involving marketing and sales, the *negdel* was the bottom rung of an organization that received its orders from the central state administration. In Ulaanbaatar, the Central Negdel Association and the Ministry of Agriculture determined the nation's livestock and animal product needs for food, factories, and export, and established the prices for these products. Production targets and prices were set and apportioned between the provinces based on the number of livestock each contained. The Executive Committee of each province, in turn, converted these into production targets for each of their *negdel*. Finally, each *negdel*'s general committee converted these into specific production targets for each type of animal. This was all done without markets, commodity exchanges, private traders, or even private retail stores. The entire system, from nationwide macro-planning to local micro-production, was centrally controlled and operated. Some local flexibility was possible, but in general the *negdel*'s production targets were all set in accordance with the state economic plan for that year.

Payments, moreover, fluctuated in accordance with political and ideological goals rather than any objective system of supply and demand. For example, *negdel* that did not fulfill their production targets were given goods and cash sufficient to meet their member's basic needs. Technically, these were loans to be repaid, but many inefficient *negdel* repeatedly ran up large deficits that were simply allowed to accumulate. This policy guaranteed all *negdel* (and therefore herders) a secure, basic standard of living without having to worry about successful production or market fluctuations.

We spent a lot of time talking to nomads about how their *negdel* really operated at the micro level. One conversation with several of our Tsaganburgas neighbors—Sanjav, Myxa, Basenjav, and Batarjav—was especially instructive.

"It's simple," said Batarjav, a very competent and hard-working young herder in his thirties whose skill we came to respect. "We earn most of our income from the collective animals we look after. Every year we discuss with the head of the *brigad* what consignment of animals we will herd. The collective gives us only one kind of animal to herd since that makes herding easier. This year, for example, I have only female yaks from the *negdel*, no sheep or goats. Next year, if I want, I could switch to something else, for example, to herd female sheep."

Another nomad responded that people didn't switch often. "I have kept the same herd of female sheep for 10 years now," he said. "It's much better that way, since I know these animals well."

Batarjav then added, "We look after the *negdel* animals for the year, receiving wages for the actual herding and for producing specified amounts of animal products such as wool and milk."

Nomads bring their milk to a ger *for weighing by a* negdel *official (right). In earlier years, a* negdel *truck picked up milk a couple of times a week, but in 1991 gas shortages prevented this so a "milk processing plant" was set up in a large* ger *in the mountains.*

(below) Butter is made at the processing plant.

The wage for herding pays a set amount per animal per day, and does not depend on performance or productivity. Sales of products such as wool are set by state production targets. For example, in 1990, Batarjav had to provide the *negdel* 21 ounces of yak wool, 18 ounces of yak hair, and 63.5 gallons of milk from each of the 25 *negdel* yaks he held. He was paid for each of these products in accordance with state guidelines. Herders also received payment for livestock survival and growth. For example, Batarjav had survival targets of 75% of the calves born and 70% of the adult females.

Herders, however, were not simply wage-laborers performing discrete tasks without much responsibility. Mongolia's herding collectives retained a basic dimension of the traditional production system by making individual households personally responsible for a *particular* group of *negdel* animals. After taking possession of a herd, the household managed it for the year, deciding where to graze and when to move and do the harvesting— milking, shearing, and so on—much as it had in pre-collective days.

The situation of Chimikzool, a young household head with three pre-school children who was herding female sheep, helped us to under- stand the complex way the *negdel* worked. In fall, 1989, he held 250 of the *negdel*'s fertile female sheep—those expected to become pregnant and give birth. He explained, "My task is to ensure that these females give birth in the spring of 1990, and then to herd the mothers and lambs until July or August 1990 when I turn in all the six-month-old lambs to the *brigad*." His work involved riding out with his herd to direct the daily grazing and moving camp when he felt the grass in an area was inadequate. He and his wife, Nara, also oversaw the lambing activities in spring and the milking and shearing.

The six-month-old male and female lambs that he turned over to the *negdel* in 1990 were immediately transferred to another herder who cared for 350 such lambs. His job was to fatten the lambs for a year, returning them to the *negdel* the following summer (1991), when they were 18 months old.

Sheep and goats are often herded together.

At this time the *negdel* transferred the 18-month-old (male) sheep to other herders who drove them 260 miles north to the Siberian border, where they were delivered to Russian officials (for meat). This sale was contracted by the state. The 18-month-old female sheep that were turned over to the *negdel* were also redistributed—this time to replace older and infertile *negdel* females held by different families like Chimikzool. The infertile females were slaughtered to meet the *negdel*'s quota for providing meat within the country. The *negdel*'s management strategy, therefore, involved selling all male goats, sheep, and yaks for meat, along with all infertile or sub-fertile adult females. Consequently, the *negdel*'s herd consisted almost entirely of fertile female animals and juveniles, with the exception of small numbers of male camels and horses used for transport, riding, and stud stock.

The herders had some private animals, too, and Batarjav also explained how this system worked. "Alongside the *negdel* animals," he said, "I herd about 130 private animals. These provide my family its supply of meat, milk, cheese, butter, and so forth. Until a few years ago the government permitted only 50 animals per household, so things were hard. Recently, the limit was raised to 75 and then to 100, and now this year, thankfully, all limits to the size of private herds are removed." The rationale for these limits was to ensure that the *negdel* remained the main source of herders' income, and therefore the focus of their attention, and to prevent the reemergence of large wealth differences.

Since private animals functioned mainly to satisfy subsistence needs, the herders normally kept all five kinds of animals, with proportionately more female yaks than in the overall *negdel* herd, since these are the household's main source of milk, butter, and cheese. These private animals were herded together with *negdel* animals, albeit not necessarily by the household that owned them. The normal custom in Moost, for example, was for a household that herded *negdel* yaks to also herd its own private yaks together with those of relatives and friends who were not herding *negdel* yaks. Reciprocally, households herding yaks would send their private sheep and goats to one of the households herding *negdel* sheep and goats. That way, most households herded just one species, even though they owned five. Privately owned female animals, however, were frequently brought back at the time of birth, and female yaks, in particular, were kept by their owners in summer and fall in order to obtain their milk.

In 1990, the average size of private herds was 78 animals per household, but 24% had over 100 head. The nomads paid no taxes per se on these, but had to fulfill state production targets for milk, meat, and fibers. That is, they were required to sell specified amounts of products from their own animals at state-set prices.

This older woman took advantage of the immobility of these corraled animals to pick a sheep for slaughter.

Collectivization, therefore, retained and relied upon the nomad's traditional herding skills. In a sense, it was basic Mongolian pastoral nomadism overlaid with a communist template of centralized planning and state-set production targets and prices. The independent herders became "socialist workers" in some important ways, but in others retained their traditional self-reliant nomad spirit and skills. The *negdel*'s leaders and the government decided on the overall composition of the herds—how many private animals they could own, and how many head of *negdel* livestock to sell—but the nomads were in charge of the critical everyday herd management decisions such as where to graze and when to move, albeit within the confines of the *negdel*'s territory.

The centralized production system also shared other important commonalities with the nomads' traditional economy. Before communism, Moost's nomads obtained trade goods from camel caravans that came to them from China laden with fabrics, tea, tobacco, jewelry, and other commodities. They bartered animals and skins for these at exchange rates set primarily by the traders. During communism, the "state" played a similar role, bringing goods to the nomads through stores in exchange for their products at set prices.

Not more than 9 or 10 years old, this young herder is already an expert rider.

Retired from the collective, this man looks after his private herd while collecting his pension.

Counting yaks before the drive to Siberia was an annual event until 1992, when economic disorder in Siberia led to cancellation of the drive.

Thus, though fundamentally different from traditional pastoralism in critical ways, such as limits on herd size and wealth accumulation and greater restrictions on movements, the collective economy incorporated important components of the traditional system of Mongol nomadic pastoralism, such as the day-to-day household management of herds.

Sheep and yak calves in a lush meadow take a rest from eating.

When nomads need meat, they go out and lasso an old or infertile animal from their private herd.

THE *NEGDEL* AND PRODUCTIVITY

Some households pitch two ger, *the smaller of which is primarily for storage —and occasionally for visiting anthropologists.*

THE MOOST NOMADS' SATISFACTION WITH THEIR *NEGDEL* WAS EVIDENT when we first met them in 1990—and it was easy to understand. On that initial visit we were surprised to find the nomads had a very secure existence with a satisfactory standard of living that met their needs and expectations. Basic foodstuffs such as flour and rice were readily available in the district and *brigad* shops, along with luxuries like candies and cookies. These shops were also stocked with imported products including East German sunflower oil, Bulgarian strawberry jam, Hungarian catsup, Georgian brick tea, Russian sugar cubes (from Cuban sugar), and fabrics and brocades from Russia and China. The nomads also were financially able to purchase these. For example, the occasional specialty item such as a decorative wall rug sold out immediately. A number of nomad households had purchased Russian and Czechoslovakian motorcycles, and a few even owned new Honda and Yamaha portable gasoline generators. The nomads' hospitality plates were full of purchased and home-produced foodstuffs, and in fall 1990, their parties and ceremonies were sumptuous affairs, overflowing with food. The nomads, to be sure, wanted more manufactured goods, electricity, and higher salaries and pensions, but they had a comfortable and secure life.

A look at their income reveals why. In 1989, the average household in the *brigad* we studied earned about 8,500 *tugrik* from their collective and private animals (5.6 *tugrik* equaled $1 at that time). In addition, the value of the meat and dairy products they consumed from their own animals was substantial. For example, a family of six or seven generally slaughtered about 20 sheep and goats and one yak in a year, the cash value of which was roughly 4,000 *tugrik*.

By comparison, a restaurant worker in the capital earned about 5,000 *tugrik* a year in 1990, and a young school teacher there earned about 7,800 *tugrik*. Most households in Ulaanbaatar actually earned double this since both husbands and wives usually worked, but urban households also had more expenses—they had to pay rent and utilities (about 1,500 *tugrik*) and purchase all their food.

Another way to put the herders' income into perspective is to compare it with actual household budgets. We did this in 1990 for a variety of herders in Moost and found that a household with five or six members (two adults and three to four children) spent between 1,000 and 3,000 *tugrik* for basics such as flour, sugar, tea, vodka, tobacco, cooking oil, candy, soap, toothpaste, and clothes. Consequently, in comparison with both urban residents and local standards, Moost nomads, on the average, were living comfortably. In fact, it was not surprising to learn that a number of nomad households had substantial savings accounts in the local bank.

Cash income was only one of the benefits herders received through the collective herding system. Like socialist workers in urban factories and offices, they also received vacation pay, summer and winter clothes every other year, and a variety of welfare benefits including child support payments, free education, maternity leave, retirement pensions, hospitalization, and medical care.

Many Third World countries claim to provide free education and health care, but experience has shown that when it comes to rural areas these are mostly phantom programs. In Mongolia, however, they were real. Education was also effective. The Mongolian People's Republic made school compulsory for all children in 1925, and by 1940 there were more than 300 elementary and secondary schools. By the end of the 1950s, primary education had been implemented nationally, and by 1990 there was almost total national literacy.

Trucks deliver boarding school students to their campsites for vacation.

Young children amuse themselves around camp.

To facilitate this, boarding schools were established in all rural districts, the government assuming the costs of this education, including room and board. The government further helped send children to boarding school by minimizing the value of child labor through its policy of giving households only one type of *negdel* animal to herd. At the same time, children were motivated to succeed, since they knew that if they did well in school, advanced studies and good jobs were available.

The nomad camps, consequently, had no children between the ages of 8 and 18 during the school term. The point was driven home one weekend when a big flat-bed truck rumbled from camp to camp disgorging excited schoolchildren who jumped down with their bags and boxes to walk home hand in hand with their mothers. Often arriving in their school clothes, they quickly changed into *del* and blended into the routine of herding life. Attending school clearly had not replaced their basic nomad skills.

This education system provided a path of upward mobility for herders' children and a source of trained workers for Mongolia's urban sector, which had grown by leaps and bounds during the past three decades. Good students were sent on to vocational and technical schools and even colleges, and then assigned to jobs in cities, provincial capitals, or district centers. New industrial towns like Darhan, founded in the 1960s (56,100 people in 1989), and Erdenet, founded in 1976 around Mongolia's valuable copper and molybdenum mines (85,700 people in 1989), required workers and staff. In fact, Mongolia's overall urban population increased by 983,100 persons in just 23 years. But even with the effective school system, Mongolia was chronically short of technical personnel, and tens of thousands of Russians and East Germans lived and worked in Mongolia's cities and mining communities.

This new graduate of a teachers' college was vacationing with her family when she showed she had not lost her nomad ways by helping a yak with a difficult birth.

Many Mongolians also studied in the Soviet Union and East Europe. For example, in 1985, approximately 11,000 Mongolians were attending schools internationally. This is equivalent to 1.4 million Americans studying abroad! Our nomad friend Sanja told great stories about traveling on the Trans-Siberian Railway from Ulaanbaatar to Kiev to attend his son's graduation from engineering school.

The impact of this educational and urbanization policy was enormous. We surveyed women in two herding *brigads* in Moost and found that 52% of their children age 19 or older were *not* living and working as herders. Twenty percent of these lived in district towns, 12% in a provincial capital, 12% in one of Mongolia's three cities, and 8% in the army or elsewhere. Most people we met in Ulaanbaatar, in fact, had grown up in the countryside.

Under the collective system, nomads had to sell the government fixed amounts of camel hair at state-set prices.

Decades of socialist education have made the herders conscious of cleanliness, even to the extent of dusting their ger.

Fibers are among the most valuable products the herders collect. Below, a young boy helps his father to collect camel's hair.

Hygiene was another success of the education system. Western visitors to Mongolia in the 1920s and 1930s commented unfavorably on the deplorable hygienic conditions of Mongol herding camps. Moost, however, was remarkably clean—bathing, brushing teeth, and doing laundry were regular activities. Many *ger*, in fact, had neatly embroidered wall hangings with pouches for toothbrushes and soap dishes.

The Moost nomads also had an elaborate health-care system. Mongolia followed the Soviet medical model and, like it, experienced shortages of medicines and a dearth of high-tech equipment. Nevertheless the nomads had physicians and other health specialists to turn to when they got sick. Moost's district center operated a small hospital/clinic staffed by two physicians (one specializing in pediatrics and one in obstetrics and gynecology), and several nurses and physician's aides. Each *brigad* also had a physician's assistant who had received training in a special secondary school . The physicians had a jeep and actually made housecalls for serious cases. If necessary, patients were transported to the hospital in Moost or, in more difficult cases, to the provincial capital or even Ulaanbaatar. Many herdswomen had completed difficult deliveries in the provincial hospital in Hovd, and one women we met had been flown to Ulaanbaatar for an operation on a hip broken when she slipped and fell on ice when herding. Health care and hospitalization, moreover, were free to all herders, and both children under five years and retirees received free medicines, although the range of what was available was inadequate by our standards.

That the nomads really expected these services was illustrated poignantly one afternoon at a *negdel* "members meeting" when a father fought back tears while accusing the district doctor of dereliction of duty and the death of his child by not visiting his camp promptly when called. The doctor responded that he had been on another house-call when the message arrived and had gone to the accuser's camp as soon as he had finished. This satisfied most people at the meeting, but not the father.

Hospital childbirth was another impressive success of the health-care system in Moost. Our fertility survey revealed that for decades nearly all nomad women had given birth in the hospital at Moost. "When a woman becomes pregnant," one woman explained, "she gets a checkup every trimester and arrangements are made to send a jeep a week or so before her due date to take her to Moost, where she stays in the local inn resting and waiting for labor." Women who work in shops and offices had 45 days of paid maternity leave before and 56 days after birth. Nomad women usually came a week or two before the due date.

On several occasions, we shared the Moost "Inn" with such women. It was a bit strange to see herds-women, who are usually bustling around their own *ger* and camps, sitting around doing nothing—relaxing and waiting for childbirth. Although the quality of health care in socialist countries like Russia and Mongolia is commonly denigrated—and for good reason when compared with medicine in the U.S.—it is noteworthy that the herders in remote communities like Moost had access to professional health care at no cost.

The state also helped subsidize the cost of rearing children. Mongolia had a pronatalist demographic policy that encouraged women to have lots of children by giv-ing an amazing array of incentives. Free prenatal care and delivery and maternity leave were just the first bene-fits. Right after delivery, mothers received a payment from the government called "cradle and milk" money, and, when the baby reached six months of age, received a "survivorship" payment. Mothers also received annual cash benefits if they had more than four children under the age of 16, and were eligible for early retirement. And women received medals for high fertility—the "First Order of Glorious Motherhood" was awarded to women who raised eight or more children past the age of 15, while the "Second Order of Glorious Motherhood" was awarded to women who had raised five to that age. Women were proud of this and would dig into their suit-cases to find their medal when we took a Polaroid family photo as a going away gift. It is, therefore, not surprising that a quarter of Moost women had 10 or more births!

Visits from grandchildren and children living in the cities maintain family solidarity.

Negdels used medals and awards to motivate workers. This woman proudly wears the "Order of Supreme Motherhood, 1st grade," which she earned by bearing eight or more surviving children.

Older herders fear they will lose their pensions when the market economy is implemented in full. Many asked us about the situation of the elderly in America.

Finally, Mongolia's amazing pension system was a large part of the reason for the herders' positive attitude toward the *negdel* and socialism. Unlike other Third World countries, Mongolian herders, both male and female, received government retirement pensions. Male herders received this at age 60 if they worked 25 years for the *negdel* and at 55 if they worked 32 years. Women received pensions at age 55 if they worked 20 years, but could retire as young as 36 years of age if they had four children and had worked 20 years. Herders who continued to take *negdel* animals after retiring received income from salary *and* pensions—full payment from the larger of the two incomes and half payment from the other. A new law in 1990 permitted them to receive full payment for both.

Pensions varied depending on the number of years worked and the herder's final salary, but on the average, were adequate, if not generous. For example, in Hojirt Brigad in 1989, retirees received an average pension income of 1,400 *tugrik* a year in addition to the food and products their own private herd provided. This was within the 1,000 to 3,000 *tugrik* subsistence budget mentioned earlier for households with five or six members. And if ill health forced an elder to join a child's household, the elder kept his or her pension. Pensions, therefore, were something all the herders anticipated and considered a fundamental entitlement. Indeed, one of the first questions posed to us was that of a 60-year-old woman who asked if rural women in the U.S. receive pensions. These benefits and services placed Mongolia far ahead of other Third World nations such as China and India.

Markers are used to differentiate private and collective animals. This woman cuts the thread she used to sew a marker onto her

sheep's ear. Another way of marking one's private animals is to paint one or both of their horns.

Since the state was providing such excellent benefits to the herders, it seemed surprising that Mongolia's leaders were so intent on quickly discarding the collective system and implementing a free market economy. The answer, we discovered, was relatively simple—Mongolia's own economy was not sufficiently productive to support this cradle-to-grave welfare system. The nation's standard of living had been artificially maintained through external subsidies from its benefactor, the Soviet Union. Expert sources assert that these subsidies were approximately $800 million (U.S.) a year—a whopping $400 per Mongol! The magnitude of this subvention is seen in Mongolia's cumulative debt to the Soviet Union. In 1990, when Mongolia became a democracy, it owed the Soviets 10 billion rubles which, at the official ruble exchange rate of the time, was equal to about six billion U.S. dollars.

The collapse of the Soviet economy, therefore, left Mongolia on her own and in desperate straits, and forced the country to come to grips with the real productivity (or lack of it) of its command economy. Mongolia would have to compete successfully in international trade or rapidly devolve to a state of backwardness. As Tsogt, the Minister of Trade, explained in a newspaper interview, this will not be easy. "Today," he said, "we have the potential of producing $400 million worth of export goods, but in order to meet the former import needs, we have to buy $ 1.2 billion worth of goods, which is totally beyond our possibilities."[1]

Two friends help a herdswoman repair her tent-covering on a warm fall afternoon.

1. *The Mongol Messenger*, November 3, 1992, p. 3.

The reason for the low productivity was not immediately clear to us, so we discussed the issue with many nomads and officials, including a former *brigad* leader who stopped by our *ger* in 1990. He had retired the year before due to serious injuries sustained in a motorcycle accident but was already tooling about the countryside on his new bright red bike. After serving him our hospitality plate, we asked why so many officials were complaining about the poor performance of the herding collectives. "The state has production targets, and payments seem related to performance," we said. "So what is the problem?" Slowly shaking his head, he replied, "What you say is true in theory, but it didn't work so well in practice. We used to be very easygoing. For example, there was no large penalty for under-fulfilling state production targets, and the high wages paid for herding remained the same even if a herder's performance with regard to targets [such as wool] was mediocre or poor. So receiving a slightly lower payment for under-fulfilling a target did not threaten his basic subsistence." Another official later added that state targets were set low so that all the herders could easily meet them.

Nomads still make their own rawhide rope for lariats and horse tack in the traditional manner.

Herders, therefore, did not have to excel in order to have a satisfactory subsistence. Average performance could generate enough income to secure the basic manufactured and food products they needed. The collective system provided nomads with a reasonable livelihood and a cradle-to-grave welfare system without insisting on high productivity. In fact, as mentioned above, it actually encouraged low overall productivity in many ways.

To understand how the system operated to stifle productivity, it is necessary to understand the system of remunerating herders. Consider the following case of two households each herding 211 fertile female sheep.

One of the products the negdel's *milk-processing unit made was a dried cheese that had been sweetened with sugar.*

As part of their *negdel* obligations, both households had to meet a variety of production targets, including milk, meat, wool, cashmere, and babies. If they fulfilled a target, they were paid a 10% bonus in addition to the state-set price per unit. If they under-fulfilled the target, they were required to pay the collective the equivalent price per unit they were short.

Table 1 on the following page reveals, however, that the household that met all these targets received 488 *tugrik* in income while the household that was 10% below target received 356 *tugrik* in payment (after it paid the penalties). This was 37% less than the more productive household. However, both households earned 1,975 *tugrik* as herding salary for the year. Thus, the 136 *tugrik* difference in pay for the dairy products was only a small portion of the total income (6%). And since a herding family of six could subsist satisfactorily on a cash income of between 1,000-3,000 *tugrik* a year, the lower payment for under-fulfillment was not a very important deterrent, particularly since manufactured goods were very scarce and additional income was not easily converted into desired material goods.

Wages, moreover, were paid even if the *negdel* had a very bad year, since the government provided loans to collectives in such circumstances. Furthermore, the penalty for under-fulfilling a target could often be circumvented by claiming that the shortfall was due to circumstances beyond one's control. For example, one old herder told us, "If a sheep I'm herding dies, I call the *negdel*'s veterinarian and ask him to verify that it died of natural causes for which I am not responsible."

A boy looks after his neighbor's infant son while some goat kids too young to go with the herd wander about.

Another source of lowered productivity was the outgrowth of the distinction between private and collective animals. Although these were herded side by side and were marked by different types of brands to prevent switching, this still occurred with newborns that were yet to be branded. For example, a herder whose private lamb had died might switch this with a live collective lamb, claiming the deceased lamb belonged to the collective. The lamb would be suckled by a ewe from his private herd whose own lamb had died.

TABLE 1. How the old (pre-1986) "basic" system of compensation failed to encourage productivity: Comparing the income of a household (A) that met its production target of dairy products for the year and a household (B) that fell 10% below its production target shows a small (6%) difference in total income from dairy sales from a herd of 211 ewes.

HOUSEHOLD	MILK (0.2 TUGRIK /LITER)*	BUTTER (3 TUGRIK /KG.)	CREAM (1.5 TUGRIK /KG.)	AROOL CHEESE (1.5 TUGRIK /KG.)	INCOME FROM SALES	INCOME FROM DAIRY SALES INCLUDING BONUS FOR MEETING OR PENALTY FOR FAILING TO MEET TARGET	HERDING SALARY	TOTAL INCOME FROM DAIRY SALES INCLUDING BONUSES AND HERDING SALARY
A (MEETS TARGET)	234 TUGRIK	69	24	117	444 (+11%)**	488 (+37%)**	1,975	2,463 (+6%)**
B (10% BELOW TARGET)	211	63	21	105	400	356	1,975	2,331

* The *negdel* used the metric system in its calculations.   ** This is the percent of income higher than household B.

These inefficiencies were fostered by the government's ideological commitment to eliminate capitalist competition and exploitation by removing the profit motive and market mechanisms. The goal of the communist command economy system was to avoid income disparities and class hierarchy while still producing efficiency and productivity. The motivation for hard work and improvement was to come from internalizing socialist values and "socialist competition."

Socialist competition was based on the belief that greater work and productivity could be fostered not by encouraging competition for more money, but by "social acclaim"—for socialist medals, titles, and honors and prizes like trips to Ulaanbaatar. This system certainly motivated some herders to work hard, but on the whole it was not very successful. By not institutionalizing higher standards and effective disincentives/incentives, the difference in quality of life between those who over-fulfilled and those who under-fulfilled was not that great. And the notion that there should not be a "poor class" meant that even the lazy and incompetent herders were by definition to be protected adequately by the system. Not surprisingly, when economic productivity became important to the government, several collective leaders complained to us that many nomads were lazy and didn't want to assume responsibilities or risks.

The consequence of this system was mediocre productivity: herders who could subsist adequately while expending less than full effort. The collective system succeeded in eliminating the great disparities in income and material possessions of the pre-communist society, but it failed to enhance productivity or herd growth. Mongolia had 23,834,000 head of livestock at the beginning of the full collective era in 1965, but only 25,500,000 head 25 years later in 1990.[2]

Nomad children play with goat kids much as American children play with puppies.

2. The blame for this, however, does not rest solely with the herders, since the state culled herds vigorously for meat. In Moost, for example, with the exception of juveniles and breeding stock, there were no male sheep, goats or yaks. Meat targets were sometimes so high in Moost that even fertile female animals were used to meet quotas. Restrictions on the size of private herds were certainly also partly to blame.

Despite the inherent problems in overall productivity, most herders were satisfied with their situation. They wanted a higher standard of living (more consumer goods and even electricity), but were not hostile toward socialism, the Revolutionary Party, or the *negdel*, which they felt had treated them well. A few thought that they probably could do better without *negdel*s, but we were surprised at the strong support the Revolutionary Party had among the herders.

An incident regarding the perks of the Revolutionary Party's "party secretary" illustrates this. When Mongolia became a multiparty democracy in 1990, the democratic movement insisted that the party secretaries throughout the country should give up special privileges and return property received from the government. In Moost, this question was raised at a Member's Meeting when the disposition of the party secretary's jeep, video, and animals was debated for nearly an hour. A number of herders strongly criticized the party secretary. One herder said he was no different than anyone else and shouldn't have special privileges. "He doesn't need a jeep." he said. "If he wants to go out and propagandize, then let him ride on horseback like everyone else." The audience laughed heartily at this. The party secretary responded emotionally to such criticism, saying, "Yes, we made many mistakes in the past, but still we [the Revolutionary Party] have run Mongolia for the past 70 years and we are the ones who have given you the prosperity you now have."

Herders load dry yak dung onto a camel for shipment to their winter campsite, where it will be stored for later use as winter fuel.

*A young girl sits in the sun, dwarfed by
her family's huge hill of yak dung.*

Listening to the discussion,
we thought the nomads would vote
to take back all the secretary's extra
possessions. To our surprise, however, the vote was overwhelmingly
to let the party secretary keep his
property, although not the animals.
When we asked several herders
why they voted for this, they all
responded similarly. "This is a
small matter," a friend explained.
"I would be embarrassed to be
ungrateful and take away the
party's jeep after all it has done
for Mongolia and us. Let him have
the jeep and video."

*Children help out by carrying dry yak
dung for the fire.*

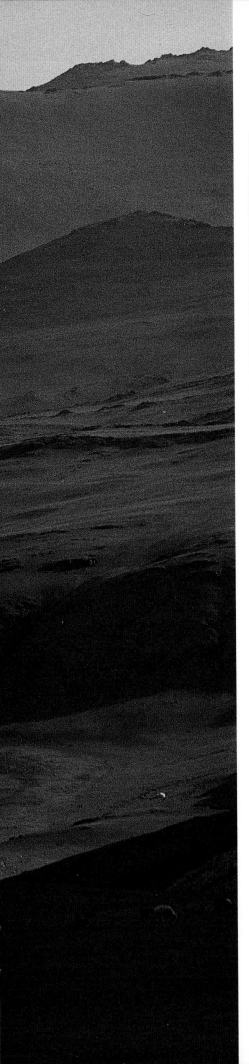

TINKERING WITH SOCIALISM~THE FIRST REFORMS

THE ECONOMIC DISINTEGRATION OF THE SOVIET UNION IN THE 1980S dramatically changed the situation for Mongolia. The issue for the new leaders in Ulaanbaatar was not whether to change, but how to change.

Beginning in the mid-1980s, Mongolia's government began to take measures to increase the efficiency of the collective system by providing greater material incentives for productivity and by shifting more animals from the *negdel* to the private sector. Although "socialist competition" with its prizes and medals continued, in 1986 the basic system of herding remuneration described in the last chapter was overhauled. In 1988 a new voluntary "contract" system (*geley*) was begun and a year later a more substantial voluntary "lease" system (*arrend*) was introduced. Reformers in the capital saw these as intermediary steps in the transition to a market-oriented pastoral economy.

THE NEW "BASIC" SYSTEM

The new "basic" system of remuneration tried to link financial incentives more closely with productivity. The amount paid for fulfilling state production targets was divided into two parts—a lower fee for fulfilling the first 70% of the target and a higher fee for fulfilling the remaining 30%. It also offered two bonus payments for over-fulfilling the target. Table 2 on the following page illustrates how this operated.

THE "CONTRACT" SYSTEM

The "contract" system introduced in 1988 offered even more financial rewards if herders contracted with the *negdel* to fulfill one or all of their production targets at levels higher than the "basic" system. For example, in 1990, the "basic" target for producing lambs was 93 from every 100 fertile females, but the "contract" target was 98. A herder opting for the higher target could earn more income and in some cases keep lambs in excess of the production target, but there was risk. He had to make up the difference from his own resources if he failed to meet the higher target.

TABLE 2. How the new (1986) "basic" system encouraged productivity: Comparing the income of a household (A) who met its production target for producing lambs from a herd of 100 fertile female ewes, with one that failed to meet them (B), or exceeded them slightly (C), or significantly (D).*

HOUSEHOLD	TARGET NUMBER OF LAMBS	ACTUAL NUMBER OF LAMBS PRODUCED	BASIC SALARY		BONUS PAYMENTS			TOTAL INCOME FROM BASIC SALARY AND BONUS PAYMENTS FOR PRODUCING LAMBS
			FIRST 70% OF TARGET PAID AT 3.18 *TUGRIK* /LAMB	REMAINING 30% OF TARGET PAID AT 8.93 *TUGRIK* /LAMB	NUMBER OF LAMBS OVER 100% OF THE TARGET PAID AT 13.39 *TUGRIK* /LAMB	IF THE NUMBER OF LAMBS IS BETWEEN 101~104% OF THE TARGET, PAYMENT IS 1.79 *TUGRIK* FOR ALL LAMBS PRODUCED	IF THE NUMBER OF LAMBS IS 105% OF THE TARGET OR MORE, PAYMENT IS 4.47 *TUGRIK* FOR ALL LAMBS PRODUCED	
A	93	93	65 LAMBS X 3.18=207 *TUGRIK*	28 LAMBS X 8.93=250 *TUGRIK*	0	0	0	457 *TUGRIK*
B	93	79 (85%)	65 X 3.18=207	14 X 8.93=125	0	0	0	332 (-27%)
C	93	96 (103%)	65 X 3.18=207	28 X 8.93=250	3 X 13.39=40	96 X 1.79=172	0	669 (+46%)
D	93	102 (110%)	65 X 3.18=207	28 X 8.93=250	9 X 13.39=121	0	102 X 4.47=456	1037 (+126)

* data from Moost records

The "contract" system, however, continued paying substantial fees simply for herding, so the payoff for greater risk was not that attractive. For example, one nomad we knew fulfilled his 98% lamb target and earned 2,816 *tugrik*. Had he been on the basic system and performed the same, he would still have earned 2,300. An even bigger problem with this innovation was the way it restricted herders from keeping animals produced in excess of their targets. The "contract" agreement anachronistically retained the anti-private herd mentality of the traditional collective movement by stipulating that herders could keep all the excess animals they purchased only if they owned less than 50 private animals. If they had between 50 and 80 private animals, they could keep half, and if they had 80 or more private animals, they could keep no excess animals—the *negdel* paid them extra *tugrik* for the excess babies. This restriction was unattractive to the most competent herders who wanted to increase their private herds, not earn more cash. The new herding option was not well received.

THE "LEASE" SYSTEM

The more ambitious "lease" system was implemented just one year later, in 1989. It sought to reduce livestock loss, increase the volume of animal products, and improve productivity by making herders more responsible for the animals they herded. Its main innovation was eliminating the herding salary.

Under this system, herders "leased" their animals from the *negdel* for a specified period of time—one year in 1989 and 1990, and five years in 1991. They paid the *negdel* a "lease fee" for each animal and received payments from the *negdel* for performance—for providing products such as wool, for producing babies, and for increasing the weight of the animals. The *negdel* no longer provided free hay, corrals, veterinary services, and transportation as it did for those on the "basic" system, and shortfalls had to be made up in kind from the herders' private animals. However, all animals in excess of the target could be kept regardless of how many private animals the family had. Sixteen households (12%) agreed to try this system in 1989.

The "lease" system was a substantial improvement over the earlier systems since it clearly linked reward to what herders actually produced. However, the essence of the collective system continued since payments were still driven by arbitrary state-set targets that bore no relation to any market reality. Was Bayerhu's (see the box on the following page) additional productivity really worth over 17,000 *tugrik* or did the state set lease fees too high in order to give incentives for change? With no market, no competition, and no free sales, there was no way to know.

These innovations were designed in part to increase productivity and in part to prepare the herders for a market economy. However, because so few volunteered for them, they did not have any measurable impact on overall collective productivity, and in any case, had dubious economic rationality owing to the high prices they were paid. Symbolically, however, they were important since they allowed a group of herders to earn very large salaries. Making large profits from work or sales was something socialism viewed pejoratively, so the changes trumpeted a new message—that herders could become well-off if they were productive, and it would be perfectly acceptable. Nevertheless, making large profits was something most herders still viewed negatively, and the rich nomads of 1990 and 1991 were careful not to flaunt their wealth.

Simultaneous with implementing these reforms, the government set production targets for private animals that were lower than those of *negdel* animals, while at the same time paying higher prices for private products. This angered many pro-*negdel* herders and officials who felt it was an attempt to give the impression that herding privately was preferable to staying in the *negdel*.

One of the easiest ways to separate new mounts is to confine the entire herd in a corral and then lasso the selected horses. However, most campsites do not have corrals such as this, so the roundup is usually a raucous event.

RAISING HORSES ON THE "LEASE" SYSTEM, 1989-90

Bayerhu, a 43-year-old herder with eight children and a 44-year-old wife (who was already on pension), raised horses for the *negdel*. He leased 433 horses (including 95 mares), agreeing to return 97% (424) of the original animals, plus colts from 87% of the mares (83 colts). This was much higher than the "basic" system's target of 67 colts. He was paid 130 *tugrik* for each colt, so he received 10,790 *tugrik* for the 83 that comprised his target. All 95 mares gave birth, and none of the 95 colts died, so he kept 12 (excess) colts for his private herd. Similarly, no mares died, so he also kept the nine mares that exceeded the number he had to return to the *negdel*.

Bayerhu was also obligated to turn over 26 gallons of milk from each mare at a price of 3.08 *tugrik* per gallon, so he received 7,600 *tugrik* for milk (80

tugrik per mare times 95 mares). He was also required to provide eight ounces of horse "wool" and 11.2 ounces of horse hair (mane and tail) from each horse, excluding the colts. He was paid 195 *tugrik* for the horse "wool" and 357 *tugrik* for the hair. His total cash income, therefore, was 18,942 *tugrik*. After paying the lease fees of 10,825 *tugrik* to the *negdel*, his net income was 8,117 *tugrik*. However, the excess colts and adults he kept were worth another 9,300 *tugrik*, and he earned about 1,500 to 2,000 *tugrik* from filling production targets from his private herd, so his total net profit was almost 20,000 *tugrik*—a high salary in Ulaanbaatar. Thus, if one could produce animals in excess of the targets, the "lease" system was a very lucrative alternative.

The nomads' horses include a range of colors, but the chestnut-colored ones are preferred.

The nomads, consequently, experienced reforms in the late 1980s, albeit optional ones. They knew that Mongolia was changing, but still felt secure in the structured world of their *negdel*. They did not understand clearly why their comfortable way of life had to be discarded for a market economy, something they correctly interpreted as a euphemism for capitalism— a system they had been taught for 70 years to view as exploitive and cruel. Instead of explaining the extent of Mongolia's dependence on Soviet aid and the impossibility of continuing socialist economics, the government had simply asserted that Mongolia needed a market economy so that Mongolians could have a better standard of living. This puzzled many herders who felt they already had decent lives, and also raised the unrealistic expectation that the new government would quickly increase the flow of manufactured goods and services.

The herders, therefore, were basically satisfied with their situation. There was some anxiety, but they did not think the changes would radically degrade their standard of living. Flour, sugar, and cooking oil were abundant, as were clothing, fabrics, felt, boots, and so forth. The local store had even received several shining new Yamaha gasoline generators in 1990, which were immediately snapped up. The herders were discussing the merits of privatization and the meaning of the mysterious "market economy" while hoping for a mild winter, high state prices on the next year's production targets, and still greater availability of manufactured goods. They talked about a Mongolia without *negdel*s and speculated where or how they would "find markets" for their milk, meat, and fibers, but these issues seemed distant.

A few nomads felt that eliminating the *negdel* would be good. As one put it to us, "If I can get my share of the *negdel*'s animals, I am ready to go it alone. I don't need them to tell me how to herd." But in general, the herders were negative or simply unsure about the proposed changes. One 73-year-old pensioner aptly conveyed this view when he told us, "Maybe the free market is better for Mongolia, but we cannot start it right away. We need time to learn about how the market system works and how we as nomads will operate under it. Things must be introduced gradually."

Among the biggest concerns of the nomads was the potential loss of entitlements they associated with *negdel* membership. Many feared that eliminating the collective system would mean they would have to pay for their own health care and education and would lose their pensions. *Negdel* officials appeared to be encouraging such fears by warning nomads that in market economies like the U.S. people pay very high taxes. Their hope was that most herders would choose not to herd privately when the time came to privatize.

Some herders were also expressing genuine concerns about a return of exploitation and poverty if a market economy were implemented. At the members' meeting mentioned earlier, a young herder passionately said, "In the market system the more capable will do well and take advantage of it and become rich, and those who are less capable will become poor. We have to watch out that we don't return to the past feudal system."

An outsider might travel for hours or days in the Altai Mountains without seeing ger, *but locals have names for hundreds of campsites and know when they are occupied.*

Otgon, a 78-year-old widow, moved in with her daughter and son-in-law when she could no longer manage on her own. She remains active doing tasks around camp.

Many herders expressed similar concerns, for example, that if the *negdel* was disbanded the rich herders would start hiring the poor to herd, returning to the old days. One official told us, "We here do not like the idea of returning to having laboring slaves. We know this is what happened in Inner Mongolia (in China) after communes were ended [in the 1980s], and that is why we are opposed to simply ending the collective." We asked Altyngiril, chairman of the *negdel*, about the possibility of rich nomads hiring poor herders to do all the work, and he asked us what the herders were saying. When we said they spoke negatively of this, his face broke out in a triumphant smile and he said, "Yes, we here do not like hiring others as laborers—it is a step backward to the old system."

The government, itself, was concerned with the fate of the incompetent and poor under the coming market economy and tried, with little success, to help them increase their private herds in advance of the changes. As the local brigade chief told us, "We have been giving some of the poorest households free animals to build up their private herd, but it hasn't been effective since these households generally eat or sell them immediately."

Makeshift toys help children pass the time.

So despite some government warnings that gasoline might be in short supply in the coming year and that the herders should return to the old way of moving camp by camels rather than trucks, rapid change did not seem imminent. Mongolia had become a democracy, but the change was bloodless, and the Revolutionary Party had won decisively in the first election. All the local elected officials were Revolutionary Party members whom the herders knew and trusted.

At this point, in mid-November 1990, the nomads began to scatter to their winter campsites, and the first phase of our research came to an end. When we said our good-byes to the herders, explaining that we would return the following May, neither we nor they appreciated how quickly and how drastically their world was about to change, nor that we had just witnessed the end of an era.

(opposite) Older siblings are caring and indulgent of younger brothers and sisters. (this page, top) A pensioner and his neighbor beat the authors soundly at the Mongolian version of gin rummy. (above) newlyweds in their wedding finery

1991~
THE TRANSITION BEGINS

ON JANUARY 1, 1991, THE SOVIET UNION BEGAN A NEW TRADING POLICY with its former socialist "brother" nations. All trade within the former socialist bloc was to take place at world-market prices in hard currency. Previously, trade had been regulated by "Comecon," the U.S.S.R.-led communist bloc economic organization that organized multilateral long-term cooperative programs in the areas of transportation, food, energy, and consumer goods.[1] Roughly 94% of Mongolia's exports and 97% of its imports were with Comecon countries. Member nations in Comecon did not have to worry much about markets or competition or quality, and there was a barter-like quality to the system. Now, however, Mongolia had to pay for Russian oil, manufactured goods, foodstuffs, and machinery in hard currency, not rugs, meat, and horses, and Mongolia's exports had to compete on the world market.

The Russians, moreover, were unwilling to write off Mongolia's huge past debt or subsidize current budget deficits. Even more destabilizing was the fact that Russia could not adequately provide Mongolia with industrial goods such as gasoline, replacement parts, and construction materials, or with consumer goods such as tea and flour, even for payment in hard currency.[2] For a country almost totally dependent on the Soviet economy—85% of its foreign trade had been with the U.S.S.R.—this was a potential disaster.

Adding to these tremendous problems was the depressed state of the world market for wool, one of Mongolia's important exports, and a very poor Mongolian wheat crop that caused a shortfall in flour, a staple food.

---

1. Comecon (the Council for Mutual Economic Assistance) was founded in 1949 to promote economic cooperation among socialist nations. Mongolia joined in 1962. Other socialist countries in Comecom were the U.S.S.R., East Germany, Hungary, Bulgaria, Poland, Romania, Czechoslovakia, and Vietnam (from R.L. Worden and A.M. Savada, eds. *Mongolia: a country study*, U.S. Government Printing Office, 1991).

2. For example, in December, 1991, the former U.S.S.R. fulfilled only 8% of Mongolia's petrol contracts and 25% of its diesel oil contracts.

Mongolia's newly elected coalition government, therefore, faced an enormous crisis in its first year. It looked to the capitalist world for help, and received substantial loans and gifts to fill the import gap created by the U.S.S.R.'s disintegration, particularly for crucial items such as fuel, spare parts and flour.[3] At the same time, Mongolia's new democratic government instituted a series of major economic reforms aimed at initiating the transition to a free economy with market controlled prices. On January 16, 1991, the government passed a price-reform bill that doubled salaries, pensions, bank accounts, and the price of key items such as milk and bread. It also decontrolled prices for 41% of all foodstuffs and 33% of consumer goods.

The government, however, cushioned the impact of this by instituting a rationing system to curtail hoarding and speculation and to ensure that every citizen could purchase a minimum standard of subsistence. The initial list of rationed items included flour, rice, sugar, meat, tea, cooking oil, butter, vodka, and soap. Each household member was permitted to buy 12.1 pounds of flour, 1.3 pounds of sugar, and 5.9 pounds of meat each month, amounts below what Mongols were used to eating, but adequate. The government also devalued the currency by about 300%, taking the first step on a path that it hoped would end when the *tugrik* become an internationally traded convertible currency.

Nevertheless, the Mongolian economy plummeted. Frequent power failures disrupted industrial production and the supply of heat and hot water. Most food stores were nearly empty, and many had even dismantled their shelves. In the first half of 1991, meat deliveries to the capital were down 26% and milk deliveries were down 20% compared with 1990.[4]

In the midst of this upheaval, in late April 1991, we returned to Mongolia and our nomad friends in Moost to conduct the second phase of our fieldwork. Visually, little had changed. The hills and valleys were still starkly beautiful. But our first stop to see our friend Sanja and his wife Enka revealed the everyday impact of the dramatic economic changes.

After helping set up our *ger* at their campsite, Sanja and Enka invited us for tea. Their hospitality bowl had cheeses and *bordzig*, but there were no sugar cubes, no chocolate-covered candies, and no strawberry jam for the *bordzig*. Enka, somewhat embarrassed as she placed the bowl before us, explained, "Things are difficult this year because of the rationing and shortages, so I am sorry we can't offer you as much hospitality as we did last fall." They told us that they had enough flour from their rations to subsist if they "tightened their sash" a bit —as the Mongolian version of this saying goes—but at the same time their rations for flour and sugar were only about 60% of what they had consumed the previous year.

3. In 1991, a group of 14 nations and five international organizations, the Mongolian Assistance Group, met in Tokyo and pledged U.S. $155 million in aid. That group met again in Tokyo in 1992 and pledged U.S. $320 million in aid for 1992 and 1993.

4. *Mongolian Messenger,* July 15, 1991, p. 2.

While Batarjav braids a rawhide rope, his wife sews on a hand-operated Singer sewing machine imported from Russia.

spinning camel hair into thread

More serious than these shortages, however, was the Moost nomads' growing discontent with the government's policies on the herding sector, particularly prices and production targets. They were angry about many things. Their income had not doubled along with the salaries of other workers because the government had not doubled the price of the key raw materials they produced. For example, the price of sheep and goat meat had been increased only by 60%.

Nor did herders like the new mandatory lease system, which had extended the lease term from one to five years in order to accustom herders to long-term planning and responsibility. It paid herders only for market-able products such as milk, meat, and fibers. It ended payments for animal survival. It raised meat-production targets and required herders to return 2% more animals (per annum) than they had leased.

Moost herders resented being forced to accept five-year leases, and also felt strongly that meat-production targets were so high that there was a significant risk they would have to use their private herd to make up shortfalls. For example, the mutton target of 33 pounds per sheep (of all ages) was double what it had been the previous year. One very successful herder we knew shook his head in disgust in response to our question about this and told us, "The 1991 meat target is set so high that even a year with only moderate livestock mortality could precipitate a sizable reduction in our private herd. This is like a yoke on my neck. We are all nervous about a bad year." Another nomad grumbled, "We don't under-stand why the government has doubled and tripled the prices of all the things we have to buy but not the things we produce." And a third said, "What did 'going to a market economy' mean if we still have no freedom to sell our products where we want, at the best price we can get?" The herders and their leaders felt—apparently correctly—that the government had set its policies to keep meat prices readily affordable for the more vocal urban dwellers.

The herders were disappointed and angry. They loved their country and were proud of it, but felt let down by the new government. Batarjav told us that their standard of living had dropped so much in the five months since our first visit that "it would probably take four to five years to get back to where we were in 1990." Herders all over the nation began to blame the new democratic parties for this, and for the first time an adversarial relationship was emerging between the rural herders and the urbanites of Ulaanbaatar and the government.

This was heightened by the active anti-*negdel* philosophy of elements in the democratic movement. Many in Ulaanbaatar were urging the immediate disbanding of *negdels* and the division of their animals among the members. China had done this in the early 1980s with its herding communes, and from one point of view it made sense: it would end the need for separate organizations handling privately and collectively owned animals. Dorjsembey, a member of the National Committee of the Democratic Party, for example, told us unequivocally, "The policy of the Democratic Party is to implement total privatization of herds and pastures without the current system of state-set production quotas and fixed prices. We should tax the nomads on their income, not make them turn over goods to the state." The logic underlying this was simple—the quicker Mongolia does away with such remnants of socialist economics, the sooner it will become an economically productive nation.

While many nomads wanted an end to state-fixed prices, they were also dubious—for good reason—about their ability to market goods privately. So they perceived the democratic movement's attacks on the *negdel* as threats to their security and well-being. It was easy to empathize with them, for the advocates of immediate privatization did not seem to have a plan as to how this "shock" privatization would work. For example, when we asked Dorjsembey how the nomads would be able to market their goods and obtain the products they needed if the *negdel* were abolished, he could only respond vaguely, saying, "The free market will take care of this." Such answers were not very reassuring to the herders and their leaders.

In Moost, such feelings were discussed quietly in the herding camps where the nomads' basic nature helped them to accept difficult conditions fatalistically. But the *negdel* leadership objected noisily to this scenario, arguing that a rapid shift to a market economy could mean the herders' ruination. Altyngiril, conservative chairman of the Moost *negdel*, summed up his distaste for the reforms by saying, "In the past *we* [the communists] offered people seven kinds of food for the hospitality plate, but under the new government we only have four kinds of food—and given the current situation, who knows how many we will have in the future."

In June 1991 a pivotal national meeting of negdel herders convened in Ulaanbaatar. Sun-tanned herders, such as this man, attacked the government's plan to privatize all animals as well as its recent price reforms.

The collective movement, moreover, was well positioned to lobby for itself. Through the Central Negdel Association in Ulaanbaatar, it had a powerful political voice. The association, in fact, executed a shrewd preemptive strike in early 1991 by organizing a national survey of *all* herders regarding the future of the *negdel*. When the results revealed that 88% of the herders indicated they wanted the *negdel* to continue, it became difficult for the government to ignore the overwhelming support of the herders.

This discontent exploded into the open at a national conference on privatization called by the Central Negdel Association in June 1991. When we attended this meeting with delegates from each *negdel*, we heard them openly attack not only the plan to disband collectives, but also the existing government-set price structure and production targets. Several speakers threatened that their *negdel* would not fill the state meat-production target unless prices were increased. Some went further, calling for the elimination of the entire system of state targets and fixed prices, and still others demanded payment for meat in hard currency so they could import the goods they needed. The herders and their leaders were quickly recognizing the extent of their leverage under the new democratic system. The government's decision to keep meat prices low was now threatening to backfire and precipitate a nomad boycott which could result in a disastrous and destabilizing shortage of meat in the urban areas.

The highest national officials, including Ochirbat, the well-liked president from the Revolutionary Party, came to this meeting, gave speeches, and answered questions. Ochirbat's closing-day speech tried to mollify the herders and *negdel* officials, flattering them and asking for their support:

> ... *Nomads have been carrying this country for centuries and are still carrying it and will do so in the future. I think Mongolia is a nomadic civilization and that there are few countries like ours. You nomads preserve the traditions and culture of the Mongolians. . . .*
>
> ... *I'll suggest that the government liberalize prices for goat meat and sheep wool, but for sheep meat, it is difficult to do this. Just two days ago we learned that our budget deficit is 1.7 billion* tugrik. *At this time we cannot increase the price of sheep meat. After 1992, we will review this question and try to solve it. . . . So please try to make only demands that the economy can handle.*

(paraphrased from notes taken at the meeting)

At the meeting, delegates reached the agreement that *negdel* could be preserved under the guise of privatized "share-holding" companies that retained ownership of as many as 70% of the *negdel*'s animals. Individual herders could join the company or herd privately or a combination of the two. Or *negdel* members could simply decide to disband their *negdel*. Meetings of the members in each *negdel* would decide these issues. The government, moreover, also gave the impression that part of future meat payment would be in hard currency. The pro-*negdel* faction, therefore, won a major victory.

In the spring of 1991 the growing season started late, so households with a reserve of hay fed it to their newborn animals.

The herders' considerable resistance in 1991 toward the new reforms and their increasing disillusionment with democracy and the new national leadership indicated that the government's ability to resolve these problems in 1992 would be crucial. If it was unable or unwilling to create a fair and comprehensible transition policy for the herding sector, it was not unlikely that the polarization of the rural population would increase, creating the conditions for a conservative political backlash.

Thus, as we said our second farewells to the resourceful nomads we had come to respect and admire, and took a last look at the Altai Mountains, we had mixed feelings. We were excited that Mongolia had adopted a democratic form of government and was moving rapidly to develop an economy that could compete in the world marketplace. But at the same time, we felt sad that the lives of these proud and dignified nomads had taken a sudden turn for the worse and might decline further still in the years ahead.

FROM *NEGDEL*
TO SHAREHOLDING
COMPANY

THE NATIONAL ECONOMY WAS IN SHAMBLES WHEN MEL AND SHERYLYN Briller, an anthropology graduate student at Case Western Reserve University, arrived in Mongolia on July 28, 1992.[1] Nearly one of every three factories was idle due to repeated power failures and a severe lack of spare parts, and the past year had seen high inflation and further shortages of foodstuffs and consumer goods. The national deficit in 1991 was a record three billion *tugrik*, and 1992 seemed likely to exceed that.

The country was being kept afloat through substantial foreign aid, but this assistance was specifically earmarked to help weather the transition to a market economy, and therefore could not be expected to continue for long. Thus, Mongolia's leaders were under enormous pressure to get the economy moving quickly.

There were opposing ideas about how to accomplish this. The Revolutionary Party supported gradual price liberalization buffered by rationing to ensure food would be available to everyone. Others, particularly several of the new democratic parties, felt that rationing was a mistake that would only prolong Mongolia's economic plight because it inhibited entrepreneurship and precluded the emergence of market forces. In March 1992, the government decided to retain its gradualist policy of decontrolling prices step-by-step while maintaining rationing on fewer and fewer items, but further liberalized prices. Prices on most items in Ulaanbaatar shot up 75% as a result, including rationed items.

The relentless downward economic spiral made the "rapid marketization" policy of many democratic party leaders appear flawed and insensitive to the interests of the common people, so when the election for a new parliament was held in June 1992, the Revolutionary Party captured over 90% of the seats. This vote of no confidence in the leadership of the democratic movement was no great surprise to us, since we had seen the anger in the countryside in 1991, but it raised the disquieting possibility of slipping back to a single-party totalitarian state. However, the dominant faction of the Revolutionary Party continued to support democracy and the need for a market economy.

---

1. Cynthia was unable to return due to previous commitments.

Thousands attand the free market on the outskirts of Ulaanbaatar. Many items unavailable in stores can be found here—for high prices.

We were eager to leave Ulaanbaatar for Moost, but travel and provisioning had become difficult. Buying supplies illustrated vividly how serious the economic disarray had become. Without ration cards, we could buy virtually nothing at government stores. However, a parallel "dollar economy" had blossomed in Ulaanbaatar in "dollar stores"—stores that accepted only hard currency. In 1990 and 1991, these stores stocked mostly imported cigarettes and liquor, along with export-quality Mongolian leather and cashmere goods. Now they sold us as much sugar, flour, rice, coffee, soap, and even Skippy peanut butter as we wanted. "Dollar shops," however, were out of the reach of most Mongolians, who could only obtain hard currency on the black market at the rate of 250 *tugrik* to the dollar. At this rate, a carton of Kent cigarettes cost 2,500 *tugrik*, roughly a month's salary.

A number of private stores and "free markets" accepted *tugrik*, but these, too, were extremely costly. Pipe tobacco and Georgian brick tea, for example, were in short supply in the countryside, so we decided to buy some to give as gifts to friends. We hired a taxi—in dollars—and went to the large open-air "free market" where thousands of private Mongols congregate daily to buy and sell an amazing array of new and old products.[2] A brick of green tea that had cost 10 *tugrik* in 1990 and 20 in 1991, was 600 in July 1992. A packet of pipe tobacco that cost 24 *tugrik* in 1991 was 300–500, and a pound of sugar that had cost 1.1 *tugrik* in 1990 and 2.3 in 1991, now cost 63. And the best grade mutton cost about 45 *tugrik* for one pound, roughly three times the state-controlled ration-card price. The high and escalating prices were astonishing.

2. On Sunday, the market is so mobbed that one can hardly walk. *The Mongolian Messenger* estimated that 100,000 people attend the Sunday market.

But this was the city, and we were interested in the impact of these changes on life in the countryside. Getting to Hovd, however, was more difficult than in 1990 and 1991 because air travel had become undependable and chaotic. For example, the daily flights to Hovd Province had been suspended several weeks earlier because of fuel shortages, so the tickets we had carefully arranged two months before appeared to be useless. Luck was with us, however, and at the last minute the government resumed flights on the very day for which we held tickets, so we were able to leave on schedule.

Having a seat on the flight, however, did not mean quite what it usually did. Our plane was the cargo version of the twin-engine Russian Illyushin aircraft that normally flew this route, so there *were* no seats. About half of the passengers were able to sit on the wood-plank bench on each side of the aircraft, while the rest sat on the floor amidst luggage. Everyone was good-natured about this—obviously happy to get on any kind of a plane—and four hours later we arrived in Hovd, the provincial capital, none the worse for it.

We had arranged by telephone with Puravdorj, the district chief of Moost, to rent his jeep. It met us at the Hovd airport, so we reached Moost the same evening we left Ulaanbaatar. In Moost, we found Puravdorj and his family had moved from their lovely apartment to a *ger* (also lovely) at the edge of town. "It's more pleasant in summer," he told us. The Mongols' empathy with their deep-rooted traditions never ceased to surprise us.

Tulagaa was a brigad *level accountant in charge of recording and weighing animal fibers when we first arrived in 1990 (during the collective era). Cost-cutting measures taken in 1992 to make the new shareholding company profitable caused him to lose that job and return to full-time herding.*

In 1990, the leather boot factory was a successful small enterprise at the district center. A year later, it had been forced to close because it was unable to obtain leather from the tanning factory in Ulaanbaatar.

ger *on the outskirts of Moost*

Puravdorj immediately invited us to his *ger* for milk-tea and *bordzig*, and enthusiastically recounted the dramatic changes that had occurred in the year since we left. "The nation's new constitution," he related, "now permits different types of property such as private, cooperative, and shareholding. Since last year we have been promoting private ownership here, and we have converted Tuya Negdel into the Tuya Shareholding (*huvitsaat*) Company. We did the same with the old producer's cooperative that handled the products from private animals—it is now called the Oirgil Trading Company. This is a big step toward implementing a market economy."

We asked him about the food situation, and he told us that it was obviously much worse than when we first came in 1990, but that they were not doing too badly and still had adequate flour through rations. We later calculated that flour consumption, which had been about 18–22 pounds per person per month in 1990, had decreased to about 11 pounds at the start of rationing in 1991, and now was only six and a half to nine pounds. Puravdorj also said that he had made several trips to China to take steps to increase the availability of foodstuffs and consumer goods, and that things were going well on this front. It was nice to hear some upbeat news after the depressing atmosphere in Ulaanbaatar. But of course, we wondered how accurate this news really was.

PRIVATIZING THE *NEGDEL*

The main structural change in Moost was privatization of Tuya Negdel. This, we gradually came to understand, occurred through an elaborate system of government vouchers.

The national government gave every Mongolian vouchers worth 10,000 *tugrik* to be used to buy state property—3,000 *tugrik* of this was in the form of three pink vouchers for purchasing small property such as animals, and 7,000 in the form of a blue voucher for buying shares in large enterprises such as factories and *negdel*.

In Moost, a meeting was convened of all the herding households in November 1991 to decide how to privatize: whether to simply disband the *negdel* and divide its property or to transform it into a shareholding company. Given the herders' apprehensiveness about marketing, it was not surprisingly that they decided to create a shareholding company that would retain 70% of the *negdel*'s livestock. Herders would buy shares in this company with their "blue vouchers." The remaining 30% of animals would be privatized, i.e., sold to the herders using the pink "small privatization" vouchers. Overnight, Tuya Negdel became Tuya Company.

Internally, however, the administrative structure remained virtually the same. Altyngiril, the *negdel* chairman, was elected company chairman, and the other top *negdel* officials also assumed leadership positions. Like its predecessor, the company owned livestock and leased them to its members, although now it owned fewer head. The main difference between the two entities was that the company now was expected to produce a profit and pay dividends to its shareholders. To be able to do this it mainly had to reduce its payroll, so the new company had far fewer employees than the old *negdel*. There were also some cosmetic name changes such as the name *"brigad"* being replaced by *"bag,"* a pre-communist administrative term.

The actual privatization process took several steps. First, the members decided that the animals to be privatized should be sold primarily to the 1,415 current and retired *negdel* members. This was accomplished by limiting the investments of nonmembers, such as office workers living in the district center, to only one pink voucher per household (3,000 *tugrik*), regardless how many household members they had.

The next issue was whether long-time members should get a larger share than new ones, and whether founding members (those who brought animals into the *negdel* in the 1950s) should get extra shares. After a great deal of debate, an allocation formula was adopted: 50% of the animals (and most corrals) would be sold in equal numbers to members (including pensioners); 35% to members based on the number of years they worked; 5% equally to original members, and 10% to non-herders.

The mechanism for calculating this was straightforward—first the value of all the *negdel's* animals (and property) was obtained by setting a price for each type of animal; for example, sheep two years and older were given a value of 400 *tugrik*. Through this process the total value of the 12,415 animals slated for privatization totaled 6,889,300 *tugrik*.

Based on this, the *tugrik* value of a per-person share was calculated for each allocation category. For example, the 50% category to be sold to all members equaled 3,444,650 *tugrik* (half the total value of 6,889,300). This amount, when divided equally among the 1,415 collective members, resulted in one member's share being 2,434 *tugrik*. The same procedure was followed for calculating the share value for each of the other allocation categories. The share for one year of work was determined by dividing the total number of years worked by all the members into the total value of the animals in this category. This turned out to be 98 *tugrik* per year of work.

Table 3 below illustrates how this affected one family containing three adults—a husband, wife, and the wife's mother (and five children).

TABLE 3. An example of the value of shares due to one herding family in Moost district in 1992 illustrates how the *negdel's* animals were privatized. The family was authorized to receive 17,170 *tugrik* worth of livestock.

NAME OF HOUSEHOLD MEMBER	SHARE ALLOCATION CATEGORY				TOTAL VALUE
	COLLECTIVE MEMBER'S SHARE VALUE	NUMBER OF YEARS WORKED FOR TUYA NEGDEL	YEARS WORKED SHARE VALUE	FOUNDING MEMBER'S SHARE VALUE	
HALTAR (HOUSEHOLD HEAD)	2,343	33	3,234*	—	5,668
BATAM (WIFE)	2,434	25	2,450	—	4,884
OTGON (RETIRED MOTHER-IN-LAW)	2,434	35	3,430	736	6,620
TOTAL					17,170

* The share for one year of work was determined by dividing the total number of years worked into the total *tugrik* value of the animals in this category. This turned out to be 98 *tugrik*, so this share was 98 *tugrik* x 33 years.

The head of the household, Haltar, was eligible to buy 2,434 *tugrik* worth of animals by virtue of being a collective member. He also was eligible to buy 3,234 *tugrik* worth of animals in the 35% category because he had worked for 33 years. His pensioned mother-in-law was eligible to buy the largest value of animals because she had worked longer and had been a founding member of the *negdel*. Haltar's family as a whole was eligible to purchase animals worth 17,170 *tugrik*. He had 24,000 *tugrik* worth of vouchers from his eight household members so he had no trouble paying for this. His household's share amounted to 31 animals.

Following completion of this process, the proportion of privately owned animals in Moost increased 17%—from 47% of all animals at the end of 1990 to 64% at the end of 1991—although part of this increase was due to natural growth.

After privatizing these animals, the cash value of the animals owned by the new shareholding company was 18,507,800 *tugrik*. This became the starting capital of the new company. Since the price per share in this company was set at 100 *tugrik*, there were 185,078 shares. These were purchased by herders with their "large privatization" blue vouchers.

All the former collective members in Moost opted to become share-holders with the exception of about 10 households (2%) who decided to begin herding privately instead of joining the company. We asked one older nomad whether it wouldn't have been better for the herders to vote against the company, since this would have meant that *all* the animals would have been divided among the individual herders. He laughed at our question and replied, "Well, that is roughly what some were telling us. They were saying that we would have a better life if we became private herders, but when we thought carefully about it we didn't see any big benefits from going private. As I told you last year, we do not know where to sell our animal products. We are far from the big cities, and even from Hovd (a four- to five-hour drive). So while having more private animals would be wonderful, it would not necessarily be advantageous if we were unable to sell our goods and buy what we need. Consequently, we decided to privatize part of the animals but to stick with the *negdel* [the share company], at least for the time being, since it can deal with things like markets far better than we could by ourselves."

A local official's explanation echoed this. "The herders decided to remain in the company for the security. They are waiting to see how the company develops and also how the private herders manage. They were not clear how they would market their products independently and many were not convinced that Mongolia would really become a complete market economy, so they hedged their bets."

Furthermore, there was apprehension about 1992—the "Year of the Monkey." [3] Mongolians believe that the "monkey-year" brings climatic disasters—severe winters and heavy animal losses. Recent records support

---

3. Mongolians traditionally use the 12-year cycle of years named for animals (horse, monkey, chicken . . .) that is used elsewhere in Asia. Each animal year returns every 12th year, and 1992-93 was the "Year of the Monkey."

Sudden blizzards that blanket the standing grass with snow are the greatest threat the herders' livestock face. Normally, however, snows are not severe and the animals can graze on bare spots.

this. In the monkey-year winter of 1944-45, one-third of the nation's livestock (eight million) died due to heavy snowfall. Then again during the monkey-year winters of 1956-57, 1968-69, and 1980-81, bad weather led to more than two million animals dying each time (roughly a 10% national decrease). The Mongolian government in 1992 was reminding herders of this and urging them to make special preparations for bad weather by storing up large stocks of hay and building more enclosures for animals. The "monkey-year" was on everyone's mind and may have influenced the decision to stick together in a structure they knew and trusted.

Moreover, the few herders who initially decided to herd privately changed their minds after two months and joined the company. They were in a *brigad* we were not studying, so we did not have a chance to interview them. However, another herder reported what he had heard: "There were many reasons for their change of heart. They found it risky to live without the company, since it was hard to find places to sell their products. Their friends and relatives also urged them to join, since it was not good to be by themselves in such difficult times when most herders here and throughout the country had opted for joining companies. I think they also got the impression that they would be taxed more heavily than people in the company."

Another important consideration was the controversy over whether herders who left the company could take a share of its animals in addition to what they obtained from their pink vouchers. The pro-market forces in the capital insisted that herders must have this right, while the pro-*negdel* faction disagreed, arguing that they should only be given back the blue vouchers they originally used. At the time of privatization, this issue was not settled. Thus, these herders also feared that not belonging to the company might mean losing their eligibility for a share of its livestock if it disbanded in the near future. Consequently, by the time we arrived on July 31, 1992, everyone in Moost had joined the company.

Under the collective system, the negdel *oversaw the selling of yaks, the first step of which was to wrestle the yaks into a chute for weighing. When given the option of herding privately or joining a shareholding company, most nomads opted for the "company" since it would continue to market the nomads' products.*

The herders and their leaders, therefore, had carried the day, forcing the government to let them move toward a market economy within the context of the familiar *negdel* now called a company. As a result of this compromise, 64% of the animals were under private ownership and the marketing auspices of the Oirgil Trading Company, and 36% were owned by the Tuya Shareholding Company, which was its own marketing agent. Both organizations were trying to sell the same products for the same people to the same markets. To us, it would have made far more sense simply to privatize all Moost's animals and create one marketing cooperative company to handle them. The government, however, was split on what to do, and had been ineffective in presenting options or explaining what would occur in different circumstances—for example, if a herder left the shareholding company. With little understanding of the macroeconomic issues and little faith in the multiparty government that seemed to be in disarray over every issue, the herders opted to increase their private herds a bit at the *negdel*'s expense, but to retain the security of being part of a familiar organization that could organize pastoralism and advocate on their behalf.

One astute herder humorously caught the essence of the changes when he summed up the situation by saying, "In the past there was organization, now there is disorganization. In the past the herders had to work hard, now the leaders have to work hard." Having fought to allow the *negdel* to reincarnate itself as a company, the onus was now on the leaders to demonstrate that they would serve the herders effectively by being shrewd businessmen. What they did is the subject of Chapter 9.

In the midst of dramatic political and economic upheaval, the nomads maintain traditional customs—here the exchange of snuff bottles as a greeting.

Sometimes herders chase and lasso horses from the saddle.

(opposite and above) *The rich green carpet of summer vegetation flourishes during the May–September growing season. These are the only months when average daily temperatures are above freezing.*

Yaks give milk 10 months of the year and are the herder's main source of milk and dairy products. Four or five yaks can meet the milk needs of an average-size household.

Weak lambs and kids are often fed supplementary milk from baby bottles.

THE SEARCH FOR SELF-RELIANCE

TRANSFORMING THE HERDERS' COLLECTIVE INTO A SHAREHOLDING company was just one of the changes that occurred in 1992. Other reforms created a new relationship between the herders and the state. Oodos, the company's chief accountant, summed these up, saying, "At the time of the centrally planned economy, the state gave us production targets that had to be fulfilled. Now the state organizations give us [purchasing] orders which we say whether or not we can fulfill. Both sides have to agree on the amount and the price."

Beginning in 1992, the herders no longer had to sell their products to the state; conversely, the state no longer guaranteed that it would buy the herder's products and provide the commodities and foodstuffs they required. There was now uncertainty on both sides as both were breaking new ground. These new rules freed the herders from the restraints of command economics but made economic planning difficult for border regions like Moost that were far from the main urban market in Ulaanbaatar where a quarter of Mongolia's total population resides.

These changes caused serious problems for the government. First, its policy of providing all citizens with an adequate and affordable supply of basic foodstuffs, such as meat and flour, meant maintaining rationing and price controls, at least for these two items. However, prices that seemed reasonable to the government were perceived as too low by the producers, who now refused to sell to the urban sector. Second, the decreasing purchasing power of the *tugrik* made it uncertain whether the food-supply problem could be solved even by raising meat and flour prices.

The confidence of these young Mongols in the saddle contrasts markedly with their insecurity under the new market system.

In market economies in the Developed World, supply and demand regulates such situations through price shifts, but in the Mongolia of 1992, there was no apparent linkage between these. Mongolia did not have the manufacturing capacity to produce the goods needed internally, nor did it export enough to be able to import commodities. Consequently, their money had a severely reduced value—there was little or nothing to buy and inflation rates of 200-300% a year (during 1991 and 1992) had marginalized savings. Even raising prices, therefore, might not increase sales of meat. Three young teenage herders who stopped by our *ger* one night after bringing in their herd conveyed a common view on this. "We nomads have all the money we need now. I'm not worried about money. I want to build up my herd by keeping more animals, not selling them. What is there to buy with the money anyway?"

Toddlers frequently can be seen surveying camp life from the door of their yurt.

The conundrum facing the government, therefore, was how to meet the needs of consumers, given that the economy could not stimulate the supply of foodstuffs through market forces, and the new democratic institutions precluded use of coercion to force producers to supply products.

The herders had their own reciprocal problems. They could no longer depend on the government to provide what they needed and feared that rationing would end soon. A normal, money-driven market system was unlikely to materialize quickly, so they would have to change their way of doing things to maintain even their lowered standard of living in the future. Basically, they would have to find new sources of flour, sugar, tea, tobacco, and the other products they needed, and make bilateral "barter" agreements with these producers.

The nomads understood this. It was precisely why they decided to create a shareholding company and place their future in the hands of the old *negdel* and Revolutionary Party leaders. Had they voted to end the collective and divide all its animals, each would have received about 60 additional animals per household, a substantial number. But they believed that forming a company with their old leaders would be more efficacious (and less risky) for developing these new sources of products than each operating as private herders. Although the company was unlikely to be able to pay dividends on their shares, if it even broke even, the decision made sense given the ground-level realities and limited options in Mongolia. And, in fact, it worked out surprisingly well in practice.

In Moost, the three key administrators were the head of the Tuya Shareholding Company, the head of the Oirgil Trading Company, and the district chief. They were all Revolutionary Party leaders from the collective era who had worked together for years—the Tuya Company chairman had been the *negdel* chairman, the Oirgil Trading Company chairman had been the Moost party secretary, and the district chief had been school principal and then head of the district. During the collective era, the Revolutionary Party had integrated activities in Moost, and the herders wanted to retain this unified effort. Although the enthusiasm of these three leaders for a real market economy varied considerably, the tradition of cooperative action continued under the new system and they mounted a coordinated effort to take control of the new situation.

Their strategy involved reducing dependence on Mongolian factories and the central government so as to give the herders more direct control over their basic subsistence needs. There were three components:

- establishing new direct trading relationships with enterprises in neighboring countries and in other provinces within Mongolia, that is, internationalizing and regionalizing the economy;

- championing a return to traditional modes of production, for example, feltmaking;

- formulating future plans to develop new small-scale production enterprises in Moost.

The change from a command to a market economy has radically changed the economics of pastoralism, but the basic way of life is enduring.

INTERNATIONALIZATION AND REGIONALIZATION OF THE MOOST ECONOMY

The most striking example of Moost's new economic strategy was the 1992 development of substantial trade with China's Xinjiang Province. In the traditional era, before the creation of the Mongolian People's Republic, virtually all trade had been controlled by Chinese traders who brought consumer goods to the nomads via camel caravans. In modern times, the U.S.S.R. and its communist Comecon bloc partners had replaced them. Now the leaders in Moost once again turned to China, despite the deep-seated fears Mongols (including the Moost herders) had about possible Chinese designs on Mongolia.[1] But ideology and nationalism succumbed to reality in the economic chaos of Mongolia in 1991–92. While Moost is 850 miles from Ulaanbaatar, it is only 215 miles from China. China also has a booming manufacturing and agricultural economy that could provide all the products the nomads want and need, and appears motivated to do so.

For its part, the Mongolian government realized that distant provinces such as Hovd would be unable to compete with herders surrounding Ulaanbaatar because of the high costs of transportation, so it advocated the development of border trade for them. A Sino-Mongolian trade agreement was signed with China in 1991, establishing a series of border sites where locally contracted trade could occur. One such site was on the Mongolia-Xinjiang border, and the leaders of Moost took the opportunity of the official "opening ceremony" to begin trade negotiations with their Chinese counterparts.

By the time we returned to Moost in August 1992, the district chief and other local officials had made several business trips to Xinjiang Province to negotiate a major contract. Moost sold 38.7 tons of wool (half from private herds and half from the company's herd) in exchange for a variety of manufactured products and foodstuffs including 17,000 yards of Chinese canvas, 200,000 boxes of matches, and 4.5 tons of brick tea. Although the Moost officials all commented on how difficult it was to strike a deal with the hard-headed Chinese, the tea agreement portion of the agreement reveals the degree of Chinese interest in this trade.

1. We had several discussions with herders who vociferously criticized the government's plans to decrease the size of the army because of the huge national deficit, arguing that Mongolia needs more, not fewer, troops to defend against China. Although military expansion seems an unlikely scenario, it should be noted that Taiwan still claims Mongolia as part of China.

Herders are returning to traditional technology to produce many essential items. For example, factory-made felt was no longer available so herders started making it by hand for the first time in 40 years. A key step in this process is to fluff up the wool by beating it with thin sticks.

The nomads were accustomed to drinking Georgian brick tea, which is made from green tea leaves. When milk is added to the tea, it turns white. After 1991, however, Georgian tea was unavailable, so Chinese brick tea was substituted. The first Chinese tea, however, left the tea too brown when milk was added, so the herders considered it inferior. When the Moost leaders informed their Chinese counterparts about this, the Chinese assembled 10 varieties of Chinese brick tea for the Mongols to sample, and an appropriate type was found. Whether this cooperative spirit was primarily economic or political, the result was the overnight emergence of significant trade.

Moost trucks took their wool to the border and received the first shipment of Chinese goods in mid-August 1992. Other shipments were expected the following month. Moreover, another agreement, to take place later in the year, would exchange some of Moost's annual yield of 10,000 sheep and goat skins for Chinese sewing machines, fabrics, four flour-milling machines, sugar, window glass, candles, and 165 tons of flour (roughly 77 pounds per person).[2] This new China trade not only meant lower transportation costs and less dependence on scarce gasoline, but gave the Moost leaders the ability to obtain commodities that were in short supply or simply unavailable in Mongolia.

It was amazing to see the alacrity with which the former communist leaders took to trading and business, even the former "party secretary," who was now the head of the trading company. Although he still felt the government should more actively structure economic life through price controls and targets, he was energetically wheeling and dealing to trade and make profits for the herders. We happened to be on the street in Moost when the first trucks arrived from China laden with canvas and asked him about the arrangements. He was ebullient about his success in making a good deal and rattled off the prices from memory just like a long-time Western capitalist.

Trading with China, however, was not completely free from government interference. All contracts had to be checked for prices before export/import licenses were granted in order to prevent local officials from making bad deals that could inadvertently drop the price of an export item for the entire country. Moost, for example, had already experienced this. It had negotiated a contract with China to sell skins in exchange for flour that the government had disapproved because the price of 31 pounds of flour per skin was too low—the minimum was 37 pounds per skin. The Moost leaders were disappointed, but went back to China and finally made a new deal.

The leaders in Moost were not just scrambling to provide for the immediate needs of the herders, they were also concerned about the longer-term economic viability of the district. Puravdorj, for example, was enthusiastic about developing small-scale workshops and factories in Moost that could provide products the herders wanted as well as create employment for townsfolk. Buying flour mills was an example.

Puravdorj's explanation of this deal revealed his thinking. "We bought the four flour mills," he said, "because we think we'll need these in the future. I am told it is certain that all prices will be liberalized soon, so we will be responsible for buying flour for the herders ourselves [i.e., there will probably be no price controls on flour]. There is also an insufficient milling capacity in Mongolia, so we think it will be easier and cheaper to buy wheat from producers and mill it ourselves than to depend upon buying processed flour. We plan to use two mills for this and sell two to other districts."

2. The official government annual ration amount was 79 pounds per person, so this satisfied their needs for a year.

The new focus on developing trading partners was also being pursued within Mongolia. In 1992, the chairman of the Tuya Company visited a former state farm in Hovsgol Province, roughly 420 miles to the northeast, to explore buying wheat and some farm machinery. We later learned he had contracted for 33 tons of wheat that would be milled into flour at the new factories Moost was buying from China.

At the same time, Moost traditionally supplied large amounts of meat to Siberia (roughly 260 miles to the north) every summer under state agreements. Male sheep, goats, and yaks were driven live right up to the border. Arrangements had been made by the central government in 1992 for Moost to send a consignment of 331 tons of live animals, but this fell through when the Russians backed out of the deal. Apparently, the Russian government offices involved could not get the local enterprises to accept the price it had negotiated. Again the collapse of the Russian economy was playing havoc with Mongolia's ability to restructure its economy. The Moost leaders had planned to visit Siberia that fall (1992) to initiate direct trade for future years, but canceled the visit after this failure. In part this was due to the difficulties in Russia, but in part it was due to the new trade with China. Selling live animals to Siberia meant losing their skins, and it was the skins rather than the meat that China wanted, so by the end of 1992 the utility of a meat trade with Siberia was being called into question.

THE MEAT CONFLICT

The new market freedoms of 1992 created a summer stalemate over the internal sale of the herders' main product—meat. The government had established an "agricultural commodities exchange" in Ulaanbaatar (with branches in each province) to act as an intermediary in buying and selling agricultural products. In 1992, it sent Moost a "purchase order" for meat (for Ulaanbaatar slaughterhouses) but the price was too low, and Moost responded by informing the commodities exchange of the price it wanted to receive. Taking yak meat as an example, the government had set the retail price for (dressed) yak meat at 11 *tugrik* a pound. The herders wanted about 13.6 *tugrik* per pound, and the commodity exchange offered Moost a wholesale price of 9.5 *tugrik* a pound. Moost's situation was further complicated by its high transportation costs—roughly 1.8-2.2 *tugrik* per pound. These had traditionally been paid by the purchaser, but now were said to be the responsibility of the seller. The herders told their leaders that they preferred not to sell any meat this year if they could not get their price, and when we left in August 1992, they had still been unable to reach an agreement over the selling price. Thus, the future supply of meat for Ulaanbaatar was uncertain.

Herders face no technical problems making good their threat to hold back meat from the urban slaughterhouses. Unlike farmers, they are not hampered by storage problems since the animals they would normally sell simply remain in their herds. In fact, as long as their basic subsistence needs are met, herders traditionally consider more animals a sign of wealth and status, not a hardship or loss, and prefer to see their herds increase.

The tranquility of a nursing two-year-old yak calf belies the uncertainty over the future viability of meat sales to Ulaanbaatar and Siberia.

Facing the specter of disastrous shortages of meat in the urban areas, the government gave in and raised all prices on September 28, 1992, although it left a few items like flour and meat on the ration system. The retail price of yak meat and mutton more than doubled to 26.5 *tugrik* per pound, and Moost ended up selling 898 tons of meat to Ulaanbaatar and 316 tons to Hovd city, roughly 77% of what they had originally planned to sell.[3]

RETURNING TO TRADITIONAL WAYS: GROWING BARLEY

Because it had not been sown there in the past, it initially surprised us to learn that the company had decided to try to plant barley in Moost. On reflection, however, it fit the general strategy of self-reliance—of weaning the nomads from dependence on Ulaanbaatar.

Barley was traditionally the main grain food for these people, and it was supplanted by flour only after the creation of mechanized state farms in the 1950s. In Moost, the nomads traditionally planted barley part-time in Bulgan, a district to the southwest. There were no private fields in those days, and any nomad family could send a member there in summer to plant. Some households hired poor nomads to plant for them, selling part of the barley to families who weren't involved. The nomads did not perceive any role conflict between this part-time farming and their nomadic pastoralism.

3. These figures were obtained through correspondence.

Barley is processed utilizing techniques parallel to those used in Tibet, from where they apparently borrowed the technology. First, the barley is heated in a dry wok while being stirred vigorously with a piece of felt to keep it from burning. This pops the kernels much like we pop corn kernels to make popcorn. While some of these roasted kernels are eaten as snacks, most are ground on a hand-powered stone mill. The resulting barley "flour" is known as *tsamba* (the same term used in Tibet) and requires no further cooking. *Tsamba* was eaten daily in the morning and at noon together with tea and dairy products, much as the nomads nowadays eat *bordzig*.

Barley cultivation in Hovd Province did not end after flour became the dominant grain. Small amounts continued to be planted in the districts south of Moost, and a number of nomads served us *tsamba* on our first visit in 1990. Consequently, when the wheat flour shortages began in 1991, the demand for barley increased and the area devoted to cultivation began to increase. However, unlike the old days, Moost herders no longer can utilize land in other districts for farming (or herding), so Moost's decision to revive barley cultivation meant finding appropriate areas in their own territory.

Puravdorj, the Moost district chief, was quite enthusiastic about this initiative and drove us to the 74-acre site in his jeep. It was about 35 minutes from the district center in a swampy area filled with ferocious mosquitoes. The land was initially plowed by the company's tractor and had been fertilized only with manure, since chemical fertilizers were in short supply and expensive. Some wheat had also been planted.

Our first look at the site was a real shock. Puravdorj's driver pointed to the right and said, "There it is." We looked, but couldn't see any fields. We saw a lot of tall grass, but no crops. Curious, we walked out into the field where we finally spotted the barley interspersed among the tall grasses and learned what had happened. The company had planted barley but had not expended any effort to weed it! Not surprisingly, they obtained only 3.3 tons of barley and no wheat, but they were pleased because they had been able to establish that barley would grow well in Moost itself. [4]

This grandmother is roasting barley kernels over a hot fire until they pop like popcorn. She uses a stick and a small square of felt to stir the kernels to keep them from burning. Once the kernels are roasted, they can be eaten, as this woman's two grandchildren are doing (opposite, above) and ground into barley flour on a stone mill (opposite, below).

---

4. They were, however, able to salvage 37 tons of incompletely ripened wheat that was suitable for use as fodder.

(previous pages) Although vegetation in most areas is too short and sparse for hay-cutting, several low-lying, marshy areas abound in tall grasses good for fodder.

146

The district chief understood the problems and said, "This is the beginning, and we have a long way to improve. My real hope is that private households will take this land next year on a lease basis and farm it diligently." He also mentioned that they were thinking of inviting Chinese specialists from Xinjiang to come the following spring to advise them on cultivation. Whatever happens in 1993, developing an agricultural capacity is part of the local self-reliance strategy. In fact, late in 1992, Moost decided to trade their flour mill for one that could mill barley in order to make and sell *tsamba*.

Another revival involved felt-making. Felt is a critical product for herders since it provides insulation for their *ger*. It is in demand to replace worn sections of *ger* and for making the new *ger* each son needs when he establishes his own household. For 40 years, herders in Moost had obtained their felt from four large felt-rolling mills that were constructed in Ulaanbaatar in the 1930s and '40s and renovated in the 1950s. Recent shortages of power and parts, however, had brought production to a halt and manufactured felt was unavailable. Consequently, many Moost herders decided to make their own felt by hand as had been the tradition. The Moost leaders encouraged this by letting herders subtract the wool for such felt from their company production targets.

We visited the *ger* of one old man who had just completed the process and discussed it with him. He was in his sixties, and he told us that he had never made felt before, but had followed the advice of an 78-year-old woman and had made enough for one *ger* in 15 days. He was proud of his accomplishment and told us that he would be able to improve the product the next time around.

The Moost leaders also told the nomads they could use some of the sheep and camel wool they owed the company to knit clothes such as sweaters, socks, and scarves for their household, since they too were extremely difficult to purchase. Many nomads accepted this offer. Similarly, the acute shortages of manufactured medicines has led to renewed interest in traditional herbal remedies and traditional Mongolian folk medicine, which is a branch of Tibetan medicine. In addition, households that had become accustomed to moving campsites by truck or tractor now bought camels. Haltar, for example, traded a prize trotting horse for several camels in order to bring his total to five, the amount he needed to move his two *ger* and possessions independently.

Before the disintegration of the socialist state, most herders moved their camp by truck. In 1991 and 1992, the high cost of gasoline made this prohibitive.

FURTHER PRIVATIZATION AND THE INEVITABLE TAXES

Toward the end of 1992, the government came to a decision to allow herders who leave the shareholding company to take a share of the company's animals. This had been bitterly opposed by the Central Negdel Association since it was clear that having this option would encourage many herders who might otherwise stay part of the company to leave and herd privately, and this would weaken the viability of the company. In Moost, it had precisely that effect. Thirty two percent of the members now left (203 households—831 persons), taking 13% of the company's animals. This increased the total of private animals in Moost to 80%.[5] These more independent-thinking herders left because they perceived that the benefits of private herding now outweighed the risks. They would receive additional private animals, yet would have support that paralled that of those who remained in the company—for example the Oirgil Trading Company provided them the same marketing services as the Tuya Shareholding Company, and the government had shown by word and deed that it was continuing pensions and health care for all herders regardless of whether they were members of a shareholding company or private herders.

---

5. Persons leaving the company were allowed to reclaim their original 7,000 *tugrik* blue vouchers according to the following formula: 4,300 *tugrik* in animals and 2,700 *tugrik* in other assests. This amounted to 13.8 head of sheep and goats per person plus a portion of larger animals, for example, one yak went to each 8.5 people and one horse to each five people.

The breakdown in the system of state-set production targets prompted another major economic reform—the imposition of a system of taxation. At the start of 1993, parliament adopted a Law on Taxation specifying that each head of cattle was to be taxed 50 *tugrik* per year. Dairy products and fibers were not taxed. In this system, one horse, one camel, nine goats, and seven sheep were considered equivalent to one head of cattle. Households also received an exemption of two cattle for each member. A household with 154 head of livestock, therefore, would pay the following taxes:

CATTLE TAX:	4 camels at 50 *tugrik*	=	200 *tugrik*
	20 horses at 50 *tugrik*	=	1,000 *tugrik*
	30 yak at 50 *tugrik*	=	1,500 *tugrik*
	60 sheep = 8.6 cattle at 50 *tugrik* =		429 *tugrik*
	40 goats = 4.4 cattle at 50 *tugrik* =		222 *tugrik*
	Total		= 3,351 *tugrik*

HOUSEHOLD EXEMPTIONS:	8 members x 2 cattle =	16 cattle at 50 *tugrik*	
	Total		= 800 *tugrik*

Total Tax: 2,551 *tugrik* (3,351 *tugrik* – 800 *tugrik*)

This tax is equivalent to less than the 1993 price of one male sheep at the free market in Ulaanbaatar.

Fully loaded camels can carry 300-400 kilograms and can cover 30 miles a day.

*(previous pages) Households gauge when to move camp by the state
of the vegetation. Some years this may involve 20 or 30 moves.*

Although the nomad's standard of living had declined in terms of the availability of food and manufactured goods since our first visit in 1990, and although finding markets for their products was going to be difficult, they still had positive attitudes. They were pleased that they had been able to adapt to the new situation through the use of traditional customs and technology, and were proud of this new self-sufficiency and control. Even if the situation in Mongolia continued to decline, they now felt confident that they could weather the storm.

Our friend Haltar confidently put it this way: "I am worried about how we will get critical manufactured goods such as boots and fabrics to sew our robes (*del*), but we won't go hungry. We will eat meat and dairy products and barley as we did in the past. I am not planting barley now because I still have flour, but if next year none is available, then I'll go and find a place to plant barley for myself. Everyone will do that, so I don't worry about food. We were taught to wait for the central government to give us what we need, but if they can't provide it, then we can work harder and do it ourselves."

When the herders move camp, older babies usually are carried in the saddle in front of an adult while very young babies may ride in a basket. Youngsters learn early to stay in the saddle.

153

CONCLUSIONS

COLLECTIVIZATION OF NOMADIC PASTORALISM CAME TO MOOST IN THE 1950s and was only grudgingly accepted at that time. Over the years, however, the herders grew to appreciate the collective system, particularly the pensions and extensive, free, social services that it provided. In 1990, when we first arrived, they were leading comfortable and secure lives. To be sure, they wanted improvements such as higher pensions, more manufactured goods, electricity, and additional private animals—but they felt positive about their situation. Thus, most nomads were opposed when Mongolia's democratic leaders suggested abolishing the *negdel* and privatizing all animals. The idea of receiving more animals was appealing, but the risk of going it alone was daunting. They did not see how and where they would market their products, and feared that privatization would end their entitlements. Some also worried that decollectivization would mean a return to an exploitive society with an underclass of poor and hungry herders.

The privatization reforms implemented by the government in 1991-92 offered a compromise. On the one hand, *negdel* were abolished and the government ended state-set production targets and prices for most products. On the other hand, the *negdel*s were allowed to transform themselves into "private" shareholding companies similar in structure to the old *negdel* and, in Moost, run by the same leaders. The Tuya Shareholding Company, therefore, leased animals to its members just as the Tuya Negdel had done and handled all aspects of sales. This arrangement afforded the herders the continuity and economic leadership they desired while simultaneously advancing pastoral privatization by making the new "company" responsible for conducting its own trade and meeting its own expenses. The company, unlike the *negdel*, was now a profit-making enterprise whose leaders were evaluated by their ability to find markets for the nomad's products, secure the commodities the nomads needed, and generate a profit for the shareholders. These reforms also shifted one third of the *negdel's* livestock to individual herders, increasing the proportion of privately owned animals to 64%. A separate "trading company" was established to market the products of these private livestock.

When the growing season ends, the standing vegetation turns yellow and gives the landscape a golden appearance. The Mongols refer to fall as altan namar, *"golden autumn."*

Reorganizing Mongolia's command economy, however, was far more difficult than instituting democratic political reforms, and the nomad's standard of living declined precipitously in 1991 and 1992. Goods once imported from all over the Soviet bloc were no longer available and there was no likelihood of a quick reversal. The nomads found themselves with less flour, sugar, candy, cooking oil, and manufactured commodities than they were accustomed to. However, despite these declines, there was still enough food. Rationing had ensured access to key staples like flour, and the herders could consume more meat and dairy products than in the past because they now owned more private animals. A number of households had over 200 head of private livestock in 1992, and many had between 100-200. Compared to just five or six years ago, when no one was allowed to own more than 75 head, this was a dramatic increase.

The basic problem facing the herders was and is the disarray of the national economy. There was no telling when a normal market economy would emerge and allow them to sell and buy goods in an orderly fashion. Their adaptation to this uncertain and chaotic situation took two directions. On the one hand, they began to look to their past to reduce dependence on unpredictable suppliers by reinstituting traditional practices such as making felt and planting barley. On the other hand, they looked to their leaders to secure new suppliers for the commodities they could not produce themselves. To this end, in 1992, a series of trade agreements with enterprises in Xinjiang Province in neighboring China opened an important new source of food and manufactured goods for the nomads. In a barter-like trade arrangement, Moost provided wool and skins to China and received items such as tent canvas, matches, flour, and tea. This marketing success, which the nomads felt they could not have negotiated individually, vindicated their opposition to shock decollectivization—the overnight shift to private herding.

On the national level, the nomads' criticisms and threats won another major victory when the government reversed its policy of favoring urban dwellers and markedly raised the price of meat paid to producers (and, of course, the ration price consumers paid). This broke the "meat deadlock" and allowed Moost to sell over 1,214 tons to Hovd and Ulaanbaatar in 1992—23% less than planned, but substantial nonetheless. It also was an important step toward total price liberalization since it brought meat prices into closer alignment with market realities.[1]

Notwithstanding these successes, the first year of privatization also had failures. Moost did not find buyers for its 1991 stock of camel hair, was unable to establish direct trading relationships in Siberia, and, for the first time in decades, exported no livestock to Russia. The security of the old command economy was clearly a thing of the past, and Moost's herders were now part of the uncertain world of fluctuating markets.

Central Mongolia's forested areas are a striking contrast to the landscape of the Altai Mountains and a source of wood for the herders' ger.

1. This policy to liberalize prices for the remaining rationed goods, such as meat, continued; in March of 1993, the September 1992 prices for meat were doubled. First-grade mutton and beef increased from 59 *tugrik* to 126 *tugrik* per kilogram.

As a result of the changes, key local leaders were begining to adjust their trading priorities. Puravdorj, for example, now felt that selling live animals to Siberia was no longer in Moost's best interests. Russia was an unreliable supplier of commodities, so selling live animals there would not necessarily result in needed goods. However, it definitely meant losing use of the animals' skins—and these were precisely what the current suppliers, the Chinese, wanted in exchange for their goods.

Early in 1993, Moost's market transition lurched forward again with the decision that herders opting to leave the Tuya Shareholding Company could take their "share" in livestock rather than simply reclaim the "blue vouchers" they had originally used. This issue had been left in abeyance when the Tuya Company was established and was one of the reasons why no herding households had left it to herd on their own. It had been a major bone of contention since it was clear that full privatization of the herding economy (the elimination of the shareholding companies) would be difficult without this right. As a result of this new option, 32% of the members withdrew from the Tuya Company, increasing the percentage of privately owned animals to 80%.

The cold winter begins in mid-October when temperatures fall to the low teens at night. By January, lows of minus 30°F and 40°F are common.

Although commonly thought of as "hot-climate" animals, the Bactrian camels found in Mongolia have no problem with the extreme cold.

The first stage of the pastoral privatization process, therefore, had gone surprisingly smoothly. The *negdel* had been disbanded, the proportion of private animals had increased to 8 of every 10 animals, and while the rationing system continued the old practice of state-set prices for a few select items, it had guaranteed the availability of key foodstuffs. Similarly, the creation of shareholding herding and trading companies had cushioned the privatization process by relieving individual herders from the onerous task of marketing their own products, something they were clearly not able to do in 1992 given the absence of a network of wholesalers and marketing middlemen.

Consequently, as Moost's herders entered their second year without the *negdel*, they were uncertain about whether they would soon regain the standard of living they enjoyed in 1990, let alone improve on it, but they were confident they could subsist. They had experienced many changes and hardships, but were firmly anchored to their traditional way of life through their basic pastoral mode of subsistence that continued virtually unchanged on a day-to-day basis. They still lived in *ger*, still moved their camps in search of better grass and shelter, and still obtained meat, dairy items, fiber, and skins from their livestock. Although some foreign "experts" advised the government that immediate privatization was the best way to create a viable market economy from the rubble of the socialist economy, in the herding camps of the Altai Mountains that made little sense, and luckily for the herders, it was not forced on them.

It is impossible to predict how Mongolia's pastoral economy will develop in the coming years. Competing private marketing cooperatives may emerge and the traditional meat trade with Russia may be revived, but it also may well be that the present split between independent private herders and company herders (with private herds) may prove the best mix for areas like Moost. Much will depend on how factors beyond the herders' control play out. However, it seems clear that this first phase of the transformation of herding collectives has worked well. By providing the herders a very reasonable and effective compromise solution, it has lessened the social and economic dislocation while at the same time leaving the nomads well positioned to benefit as the new economic system develops in the years ahead.

However, from another perspective, the current situation has created hidden forces that could foster livestock overstocking and endanger the long-term viability of the grassland ecosystem.

Moost had 20% fewer head of livestock in 1991 than in 1965. This was partly because of periodic climatic disasters but also because state-dictated meat quotas removed nearly all male and infertlile female animals. In 1990, for example, even potentially fertile female sheep were slaughtered in Moost to meet production tragets. Consequently, if lower meat sales continue for several years, the district's animal population is likely to increase dramatically. Thousands of animals could remain that would otherwise have been slaughtered.

Exacerbating this is herders' growing need for larger private herds. As a result of the government's past pro-natalist policy, herders have large families. In Moost, the average woman over 45 years of age has borne over seven children. However, roughly half of these children were effectively removed from the rural economy as they moved up through the education system and found employment in cities and towns.

The collapse of Mongolia's industrial base has abruptly ended that pattern. There is serious urban unemployment and very few, if any, of today's herder's children will be able to find jobs outside of the herding sector and migrate to the cities. They will have to become herders. Moreover, children in towns and cities may increasingly decide to return to the countryside. Because parents traditionally were responsible for providing "start-up" herds for children, there will be pressure on them to increase the size of their own private herds as quickly as possible to facilitate these transfers. They are likely, therefore, to sell as few private animals as possible, particularly if the pattern of high human fertility continues in the years ahead. Thus, the government's policies on human reproduction are very relevant to the nomads' future.

Herders prefer large families with many children. It was not uncommon to encounter families with three or four pre-school age children.

The new administration has modified the previous pro-natalist policy by allowing national sales of contraceptive devices for the first time and by permitting abortions on demand. However, it has not yet implemented an active family-planning program to encourage reductions in family size, and has simply suggested that four children per couple is satisfactory. By focusing on maternal and child health rather than overpopulation, the new policy gives no impression of urgency. Consequently, we suspect high fertility in rural areas like Moost will continue in the near future, which, in turn, will encourage maximization of overall animal numbers. Moost officials estimate that the existing pasture could probably sustain 10-20% more animals, but this "buffer" could be exceeded quickly.

The ensuing livestock increases could quickly exceed the carrying capacity of the grasslands, and, in turn, could precipitate a spiral of ecological degradation that would be far more devastating and irreversible than privatization and the move to a market economy.

Sheep and goat are carefully skinned to preserve the fleece. Four or five such skins sewn together line an adult's winter del. *Children learn by watching and helping.*

As we said our final good-byes to the herders in August of 1992, we had mixed emotions—sadness mingled with respect and hope. It was sad to have witnessed such a sudden and dramatic decline in the nomads' standard of living. The feasts of 1990 were no more and no one thought they would return soon. An era had ended.

But it was also heartening to see the strength and resolve of the nomads under adversity. They were still unsure of where their country was going, but they were quietly confident that whatever the transition to a market economy might throw their way, they would be able to cope. Some had made the decision to herd privately, while others preferred the security of membership in a shareholding company. For both types of herders, the transition to a full market economy was being cushioned by having the crucial marketing activities undertaken by the traditional local leadership.

Ironically, while Mongolia is struggling to enter the world of capitalist materialism, the nomads of Moost are proudly returning to the simpler values of their parents and grandparents. This search for self-reliance is of course a response to the breaking down of the national economy, but it is more than that. It is a positive renewal—an affirmation and rediscovery of dormant traditions and values. Though in one sense their standard of living was declining, in another their quality of life was satisfying. Looking to their past they were finding something more valuable than Bulgarian strawberry jam.

One nomad friend conveyed this pride and confidence as we were leaving, "We will be all right. We have milk, butter, cheese, meat, and skins from our animals. If we hard work we will come out of this okay." Having lived with these proud and resourceful descendants of the Mongol cavalry that conquered Eurasia, we do not doubt that he is right. Despite four decades of socialist collectivization, the essence of Mongolian nomadic pastoralism has remained intact, and provides them the skills and attitudes they need to subsist. In fact, it seems likely that the herders will weather the political and economic changes better than urban residents because their way of life provides them most of what they need to survive and because they are producers of basic foodstuffs and raw materials whose value is likely to rise in tandem with inflation driven increases in the price of the goods they must purchase.

The transition from a socialist to a market economic system is clearly not a simple matter anywhere, nor is it one without serious risks and hardship. In the herding camps scattered throughout Mongolia's Altai Mountains, the complexities of competing in an international marketplace seem enormous. Recent changes have compelled the herders who love their way of life to adapt not only to an uncertain and often capricious physical environment, but also to an uncertain and volatile political and economic climate. They have weathered the first phase of the transition well, but it is clear that their lives will continue to change over the next five years—hopefully for the better.

(previous pages) Motorcycles imported from the Soviet bloc were popular in 1990. Shortages in fuel in 1991 led this nomad to sell his Czech cycle to someone in the district center who had a better chance of locating scarce fuel.

164

GLOSSARY

bordzig	deep-fried pastry
brigad	sub-unit of the *negdel*
del	traditional Mongol dress
ger	yurt
lam	monk
negdel	herders' collective
nirmalike	milk-vodka
suteytsai	milk-tea
tsamba	barley flour
tugrik	Mongolian currency unit

INDEX

Sheep and goats preceding their herder
create a slow moving collage.

A herd of sheep gracefully moves across a valley en route to a new campsite.

ACKNOWLEDGMENTS

WE OWE THANKS TO MANY PEOPLE AND ORGANIZATIONS WHO ASSISTED our work in Mongolia. Funding was provided by grants from the International Research and Exchanges Board (IREX) and the Committee on Research and Exploration of the National Geographic Society. The Regent's Fund of Case Western Reserve University also gave assistance. *National Geographic Magazine* provided film and processing in connection with an article that appeared in May 1993, as well as permission to reprint three maps. Larry Nighswander, our illustrations editor at *National Geographic* and Irving Somers of Somers' Photo in Cleveland, gave us invaluable advise on photography and photographic equipment.

We went to Mongolia with no prior experience in that country, so owe special thanks and gratitude to our two Mongolian colleagues —Dr. Tumin and Mr. Nyamdorj of the Anthropology Sector of the Institute of General and Experimental Biology of the Mongolian Academy of Sciences. They took us under their wings and helped us at every step of the way in Mongolia. Nyamdorj accompanied us on all three trips to the Altai, and helped as an expert colleague and as a translator. Three other Mongols from Ulaanbaatar also accompanied us to the field—Mr. Puntsag, Mr. Batjargal on all three trips, and Ms. Ganboldorma. All showed great poise and perceptiveness throughout our stays, and earned our respect and gratitude.

This book would have been far less insightful and accurate were it not for the extremely gracious cooperation of Puravdorj, the head of Moost *som* (district) where our study took place. Without his frank advice, information, and support, it would have been difficult to conduct the research. Similarly, we gratefully acknowledge the help of other Moost officials such as Bayinzool, chief of Hojirt Brigad, who unstintingly shared their time and knowledge as we interviewed and reinterviewed them. And last, but certainly not least, we offer special thanks to the herders of Moost *som*. As we visited and revisited their camps, we came to know them as real people and are grateful for the warmth with which they took us in and educated us about their way of life and made us feel like old friends.

Finally, behind the scenes in the U.S., we were fortunate to work with David Hurst at Moon Publications, who designed the layout, Magnus Bartlett and Geoff Cloke at The Guidebook Company, who organized the publication, and William McClung and Douglas Abrams Arava at the University of California Press

Mel Goldstein

Cynthia Beall

for supporting this project. We would also like to thank Stu Kollar of Case
Western Reserve University and Deke Castleman and Elizabeth Rhudy
of Moon Publications for their editing of the text, and Priit Vesilind of
National Geographic who made helpful suggestions about the *National
Geographic* article.

3002 022